# FIND YOUR HIDDEN
## TREASURE CHEST

### YOUR MAP TO WEALTH AND SUCCESS

**Matt Simmons**

This book is dedicated to anyone who doesn't believe in their opportunity at the American Dream.

And Carol, Jordan and Brad, Eric, Ryan.

Special thank you to:

A.R Elia, check out his compelling fiction novels on Amazon, Barnes and Noble, and astorpress.com.

Rick Peterson, M.D.

Gary Adams

Editor: Abigail Buckler

Cover design and graphics: Saul Fineman

Publicist, Social Media: Jordan Plunkett

Marketing and Web Optimization: Eric Simmons

# Introduction

*"How do people save for the future? We sure can't!"*

Sound familiar? Would it surprise you to learn that nearly half of America's households have no retirement savings?[1] That's close to **60 million homes!** Putting away money for tomorrow is an oversized challenge today and warns of a treacherous mountain to climb, with the apex containing your security and a comfortable retirement.

*"We have to make changes to save money, we're not getting anywhere this way."*

Our retirement years can last *decades,* and they deserve to be rewarding and enjoyable rather than spent in need. Having a financial plan in place is a *necessity* yet so many are unable to save or aren't planning ahead. Some people in this group might feel like they never had a chance.

*"The deck is stacked against us. It's the haves against the have nots."*

There is a notion that wealth is a treat reserved for 'the rich.' We will prove together that idea is *not true,* that it's quite the opposite.

There is a hidden chest of treasure available to *each of us*, and it's waiting to be discovered. While many are already on their way to financial success, others are still trying to find or follow their own map. No matter where you are on the income scale, prepare to take full advantage of a method that can lead you to a more promising future.

---

[1] USAFacts Team, "Nearly half of American households have no retirement savings," USA Facts, Apr 25, 2023, https://usafacts.org/data-projects/retirement-savings

Using this book as *your* map, we are going to pursue your financial goals using a saving and wealth building system that ***doesn't hurt.*** This method will provide you with a *more sustainable* pathway to success.

### *So, what should you expect from this book?*

Building wealth requires the ability to save, *and <u>everyone will be able to clear that hurdle</u>.* This book offers a <u>complete system that will help you to put your savings to work, building you a more secure tomorrow.</u>

*If you choose to join in, by the time you have turned the last page, you will have the foundation for a new financial future already in place!*

This is a guide to help you get the very most out of what you have. This book has your back...

*Everyone* deserves the opportunity to prosper. And *everyone can* find and build their own treasure chest of wealth and success! ***(Just like the rich!)***

*If that's of interest, turn the page!*

# Table of Contents

# Chapter 1:
## Allow Hope Into Your World

*"You can do this."*

Hi there and welcome!  Let's jump right in.  Despite popular belief, it merits repeating that wealth is *not* a treat reserved solely for the rich!!  For those among the 60 million plus households that are unable to save money to build their nest egg, it may seem that way.

That massive section of America's workforce might feel like they're fighting an uphill, losing battle.  Every month after paying the bills, they find that there's no money left over.  When they look at their bank account, it's empty again, and will remain that way for at least another month.  And then another...  They might even begin to lose hope and may feel like they're just not meant to have wealth.

Why is an empty bank account such a concern?  When we consider that our retirement years can last three decades or more, the answer becomes clear.  How can we expect to maintain the lifestyles and enjoy the fun we've become accustomed to without a source of income?  We *must* be prepared for this time.

If creating your nest egg has been a challenge to this point, what avenues have you considered that could help you begin to put money in the bank?

You may have had dreams such as earning greater income, elevating your rock band to the next level, starting a successful company, winning the lottery, receiving an inheritance, or other lofty wishes.

If none of these seem practical or certain, there is a more realistic alternative for you to consider.  It's an option that, in fact, has been *the most productive method of all in making people wealthy.*

So, what's the secret??? The key to most of America's wealth is through **investing.**[2] Unfortunately, many people feel that investing is for the wealthy.

The fact is that investing is not **for** the wealthy, but that most people who have become wealthy have done so **by** saving and investing. Too many people, <u>even those who earn a lot of money,</u> don't have enough cash left at the end of each month to save or invest.

What if you could suddenly turn things around and begin saving money? You would then have access to the investing 'club,' along with the opportunity to *multiply* your savings to build real wealth.

We're about to take care of that most difficult task, *being able to save money.* Once that hurdle is cleared, so many exciting possibilities will become available to you in the future.

While this great source of prosperity is available to *everyone,* many who are not familiar with investing might be hesitant in taking the first step. If you have no investing experience, it may be surprising to learn that 61% of Americans own stock.[3] This avenue has been the catalyst to most of America's wealth!

<u>Anyone can be an investor,</u> it's easy to get started, and we'll take care of that together right here. Wouldn't it be a wonderful world if everyone could take advantage of the wealth potential that investing can provide?? Those who have already benefited have understood that value.

If you already have your nest egg building, the ideas you'll find here *can assist you further* toward accelerated achievement of your goals.

---

[2] Adam Hayes, "Principles of Building Wealth," Investopedia, February 23, 2023, https://www.investopedia.com/managing-wealth/simple-steps-building-wealth/

[3] JM Jones, "What Percentage of Americans Own Stock?" The Short Answer, May 24, 2023, https://news.gallup.com/poll/266807/percentage-americans-owns-stock.aspx

You may be wondering what this book and system are all about. To give you an idea of your possibilities, below is a brief short story that has been written for you. *That means you're the main character!*

## 'One Small Action'

Our short story's plot has you working away in your career, but like so many others, you've been struggling to break even in your financial life. You have a bank account but it's usually empty.

It's not like you haven't made the effort. You tried taking on a second job. That left you no time for fun and didn't last long. You then decided to cancel taking vacation to put a little money in the bank. Your family had strong feelings about that idea! Your last effort was to eliminate a handful of fun activities including dining out, movies, and concerts. Those ideas were also just temporary fixes that weren't sustainable and once again you found yourself back at the starting line.

Saving money became something you knew you needed to do, but at the time was just a dream that you hoped could become a reality someday.

One fine afternoon, as you casually sorted through your mail, you were dismayed to find an outrageously high bill from your cell phone carrier. You immediately called them for help because you couldn't afford to have this happen again. Without realizing it at the time, this seemingly insignificant phone call would become the catalyst for a life-changing moment.

The helpful customer service agent reviewed your usage with you and suggested a new plan that was a better fit for your data consumption and the needs of your family. By the time you hung up, you had made adjustments that would save you close to $35 per month going forward.

You were pleased…

You decided to grab a calculator and play a math game to enhance what this change could be worth over time. "12 months times $35 is

3

*$420 a year...!"* Your satisfaction grew. "Pretty smart to make that call!" you thought to yourself.

You kept going, calculating further away from today... "Wow, that could become $4,200 saved over the next 10 years.... and $8,400 over the next 20!!" Suddenly, carrying that modest $35 monthly savings out wasn't so insignificant.

*At this point, you were enamored with your brilliance, as your initiative in making that one phone call had the potential to become a ton of money!*

**But wait. You continued the train of thought... "So, is there anything else I can think of that could further enhance that value?" Hmmm... ... ... "Not quite done!"**

Your incredible intellect produced another game-elevating stimulus you could add to your equation; "What if I *invested* that modest $35 monthly savings, rather than just having the extra cash? I mean, why not? *It's a pay raise!* What if I sent that $35 'pay raise' into an investment account every month, and put my money to work toward my future?" **(Just like investors do...)**

"What could that small monthly contribution be worth in, (for instance), 40 years when I'm approaching retirement age?"

After a bit of problem-solving, your eyes grew wide. Your analysis projected that over the coming 40 years, saving and investing just $35 per month could turn into a ***significant chunk of wealth***. (That amount will be shared in a moment...)

*The light bulb flickered brighter and was a catalyst for further action.*

You asked yourself, "What about the other things I spend money on? What if I analyzed all my expenses and created additional savings for investing in my future?"

Just as importantly, what if, in this story, you had magically created this monumental change in your financial outlook ***while avoiding the typical pain that's required to begin saving.***

4

**You kept your take-home pay intact, and you didn't have to sacrifice or give up things you enjoy so you could begin saving. Did the $35 you just recovered have any negative effect?** *Nope!*

*Our story continues with you finding similar opportunities to save within the money you're already spending. This change in your life was as close to painless as possible, since you were finding and selecting savings ideas that didn't hurt.*

*Just as you had done with the savings on your cell phone bill, you also devised a way to see what your future could be worth for each of the savings opportunities you found. You had a projection of your future worth if your investments grew as planned!*

*You began automatically packing your new savings away each month. It was quite easy, and you didn't look back. Life carried on as usual, with a new power working in the background...*

---

*Fast forward. Many years have passed. The color of your hair has changed, and the trees have grown taller. Your nest egg has also continued to grow, becoming sizable, thanks to your monthly contributions. You're starting to appreciate and be excited at how important this account might become...*

*The sun continues to rise and set, and one morning you awaken to a magical day. "Where did the time go?" you wonder to yourself. As you're driving to your last day of work followed by your retirement ceremony, your mind wanders back in time to that one small action, the little painless change you put into motion to make this day possible. You are filled with gratitude, knowing a secure, comfortable, and exciting time is just around the corner.*

*To be continued...*

-------------------------------------------------

My friends, you are about to embark on an opportunity to begin building your very own chest of wealth in the same manner your character did in our story.

(Some hands are in the air; it may be a good time to take a question…) "Yes please, go ahead…"

**"I just want to make sure I'm understanding the story correctly… Are you suggesting that by following the blueprint or system in this book, I won't need to change my take-home pay, won't need to take a second job, or make sacrifices in my lifestyle, but somehow, I will suddenly be able to begin saving and building wealth for my future??"**

**"To answer your question, *YES, you have it exactly right!*' Rather than follow the more mainstream and difficult routes to try and create savings, we are going to attack the problem from an easier angle as <u>we uncover savings that *won't hurt. We will find them within the money you already spend.</u>* This system allows you to make your own reasonable savings choices that you're able to stick with!**

Your story can have a happy ending. You'll be guided in reviewing your spending and will be exposed to dozens and dozens of <u>real and new cash savings that you can choose among to recapture.</u>

We'll then take creating your wealth a step further by providing significant research on the savings opportunities. You will be able to have a ***projection or estimate of what each of those invested savings could be worth at a date you select in the future,*** such as your own retirement age.

Having that unique ability, you could even ***customize your financial goals and wealth potential!*** *You'll have the opportunity to name a specific monetary goal of wealth, and you will be able to select among savings ideas and opportunities in this book that can point you toward your goal!* You can uniquely have a future projection of the *hidden treasure chest* you're about to create!

6

Together we're going to make saving money as simple as possible! And we won't stop at just saving, because simply *saving* money is not wealth creation. This is a book of *action*, rather than some nice ideas to consider. You will be taking part in a complete solution, taking every necessary step that jumpstarts your more promising future.

Once you have selected and created your *new* monthly savings amount, we will then *immediately*, (we're not messing around here, isn't time is of the absolute essence for you?), assist you in automatically packing that new monthly savings straight into your *new investment account* that you will be aided in creating in just a few minutes! (Note, if you are already saving as of today and have an investment account, you're a step ahead!)

**By the time you put this book down, your journey to becoming an investor will be in motion,** and you will have laid the building blocks in place for your new and improved, *shinier future.* Sound good?

Also of great importance, you will be establishing the habit of **saving** that you may have been desperately in search of.

You'll be the same person in the same situation, earning the same amount of money. Then, after making a few tweaks in your expenses, your future can be disruptively different.

Let's do a quick 'time travel' exercise: Pause for a moment and try to visualize yourself in the future, at your retirement age. What do you see?

If the vision you tried to bring into view was blurry, you're about to have the opportunity to begin repainting a brighter self-portrait, maybe even a masterpiece of your *new and improved future.*

If you're tired of the idea that investing is only for the 'rich', we're about to prove together that it's absolutely untrue! Most of the wealth in America *was created from the habit of saving and investing!* Let's move on together toward our goal!

Oh, I almost forgot… That little $35 monthly phone savings in your short story, invested over the next 40 years, at a reasonable 7.5% growth rate? *It has the potential to grow into a treasure chest filled with almost* ***$100,000….***

*And that, my friends, is how investors create wealth.*

## *Chapter 1 Summary:*

*-Our longer lifespans make it imperative to have a financial plan in place to help avoid potential decades of deprivation.*

*-Saving and investing are the keys to most of the wealth in America and are not just for 'the rich.'*

*-Making changes to begin saving can be unsustainable!*

*-Our method removes barriers to saving by using the money you already spend without affecting your take-home pay.*

*-This method can allow you the opportunity to customize and then pursue your desired wealth goals.*

*-Small monthly contributions can become large sums!*

# Chapter 2:
# Added Benefits

*"Every action starts others into motion."*

Everyone dreams about winning the lottery or finding that magical secret to having financial freedom. What if your winning 'lottery ticket' was hidden here, just like a buried chest of treasure in your backyard? *And what if you've just stumbled upon the map to that treasure?*

Here we present a method that allows you to continue living your life with as little disruption as possible. We will be using a system that is easy to enact, doesn't affect your pay or hurt your lifestyle, and will already be in place before the book is closed. You won't be asked to change how you live, or to take difficult action for your plan to be successful. *We're all about easy here!*

This is not a "get rich quick" book and there is no additional cost. You won't flip a page and be blindsided by a request for a payment or membership fee to gain access to the book's "secrets."

The disclaimer is missing too… You know; that *really* fast-talking guy who warns you in an impressive two second mountain of words that even though they're going to make you rich beyond your wildest dreams, they're not going to make any promises!?! Or that tiny print hidden in the paperwork that says there's no guarantee of future earnings. How reassuring is that???

Well, this is different… If you just purchased this book, first, that's your only expense.

Secondly, there is no need for a disclaimer or fast talk… **Because the only possible outcome of enacting the steps in this book is that you will find new money to save and invest!** How much will be up to you!

Will everyone who follows the steps in this book get rich? Of course not. Will everyone have the opportunity to begin saving and investing, creating something of value they otherwise wouldn't have had? *Yes!*

This book was written with those who are struggling to reach their financial goals in mind, *but it can <u>certainly</u> enhance anyone's fiscal situation!*

There is additional good news! Make that *great news!!!* While improving your *financial* health, other synergies will also be at work as you benefit from positive implications beyond wealth:

- <u>Security</u> is one of the primary considerations in a successful marriage or relationship. A growing retirement portfolio answers and satisfies that need.

- How would your <u>self-esteem</u> be affected if you were able to tell your husband/wife/cat/dog/father/mother/teddy bear/diary that a 'new you' has a financial plan in place to create a more successful future with exciting possibilities?

- What if you could wake up every day with lighter shoulders and the added reality of wealth and security in your tomorrow? Would you be <u>proud of yourself?</u>

- What would having a more comfortable and growing investment account do for your <u>stress level</u> or a good night's sleep?

- You are moving toward establishing a positive and meaningful <u>habit of saving</u>.

- What <u>legacy</u> do you want to leave your family or loved ones? What cause do you wish you could contribute to and make a difference? Keep reading because whatever it is that you dream about, we will work together toward getting you there.

If you like what you're reading so far, let's keep going! In our next chapter, we will clarify who is eligible to take part in this system.

### *Chapter 2 Summary:*

*-This can be an easier pathway to wealth than many that we dream of.*

*-Building a financial future is about more than money. There are priceless non-monetary benefits to be realized, including security and peace of mind.*

# Chapter 3:
# Who's Invited?

*"If you haven't begun working on your future yet, when will you get started?"*

Question: What do these two people have in common: Person A: earning minimum wage; and Person B: earning hundreds of thousands of dollars per year?

Answer: **Both can save and become investors to build significant wealth.**

So, let's confirm *you're* a good fit for this life-changing stimulus package as we wouldn't want to waste anyone's time. Are you between 15 and 95 years old? Are you earning or being paid between one thousand and one billion dollars annually? More??? Do you work full-time? Part time? Are you on disability? Welfare? Unemployment? Do you pay bills???

*If any of the above describes your situation, you are a perfect fit for this exercise.*

The millionaires among us are few and far between. Are you one of the fortunate ones? Perhaps you started a company and grew it into a thriving business? Were you a highly sought after professional? Did you receive a sizable inheritance, or did you sell property or a home that appreciated in value? Perhaps you worked hard for years and saved and invested and have *made it!* No matter how you got there, *congratulations!*

And, what about the high percentage who haven't made that list? Unfortunately, life isn't always fair, is it? Opportunity doesn't necessarily jump out and tackle everyone. You hear about the American Dream often. And regardless of whether you live in America or not, you can have a shot at attaining your dream by *becoming a saver and an investor.*

This book is structured so that before you turn the final page, you will have:

1) **New savings**

2) **Being deposited monthly into**

3) **Your very own investment account**

4) **Without touching your take-home pay!** *What a deal!!!*

*Trust that any income level, of any age, race, gender, religion, education, size, shape, zodiac sign or hairstyle can become a saver and an investor to create a better financial future.*

*Let's move on together toward that goal, we're getting closer!*

### Chapter 3 Summary:

*-Virtually any income level is invited and can participate in this savings method and become an investor.*

*-All needed steps for creating (or adding to) a new financial direction will be completed by the book's end.*

# Chapter 4:
## Estimating Your Wealth

*"Two ingredients that make investing the key to most of America's wealth."*

All the saving opportunities that you will consider in this book provide estimates of what they can be worth in your future. These projections use an average annual rate of return of 7.5%. Let's take a very important moment to define and clarify the 'Projection' and the 7.5% annual growth or rate of return.

The projections you will see suggest your potential if your invested savings grow an average rate of 7.5% annually, with each of the choices customized to fit within the timeframe from now until you retire. (You will be able to choose among 10-, 20-, 30-, or 40-year timeframes to match most closely when you expect to retire. If you're 25 now, you might choose 40 years and if you're 50 now you might select 10 or 20. And so on).

Is 7.5% an accurate number to represent the rate of return on investments in the stock market? Actually, *no.* Almost every source of historic stock market performance points to annual growth of about **10%** *since inception, including the great depression,* and the US S&P 500 index alone has averaged well above 7.5% with an 11.88% annual return since 1957.[4]

More ammunition to ease any anxiety or doubt with respect to growth in the stock market: The lowest annual return over any 30-year period going back to 1926 was 7.8%. That's what you got had you invested at the peak of the Roaring 20s boom in September 1929. You would have lost more than 80% of your investment in the ensuing

---

[4] J.B. Maverick, "S & P 500 Average Return," Investopedia, May 24, 2023, https://www.investopedia.com/ask/answers/042415/what-average-annual-return-sp-500.asp

crash and still made more than 850% in total over 30 years.[5] The suggested 7.5% annual growth number we are using is within two tenths of a percentage point of the worst 30-year period of performance in the stock market.

Now, just because the market has averaged 10% doesn't mean that you will. We'll attempt to be a little more reasonable and suggest a 7-1/2% rate of return, which more closely matches the higher end of 401k retirement fund average performance of 8%.[6] Everyone's true outcome is yet to be determined and there is never any guaranteed result when it comes to investing. But there is history to demonstrate what has already happened! And the fact remains that <u>investing has been the *key* to most of the wealth in America</u>.

Your personal investment performance shall be unknown until the final day you invest. You may realize, for instance, only a fraction of the 7.5% projection. Or you could double or triple your projection or more! Some of you could risk losing most or all your money on poor choices. And others might become multi-millionaires. Consider the 7-½% as a reasonable average or suggestion as to what may be achieved.

There are other factors that could affect your growth rate including inflation, risk reduction as we age, and more. Those are not considered in the 7-½% growth projection.

There is never a guaranteed result with investing, as everyone will be choosing their individual paths, and there is no assurance that tomorrow's growth will follow history. We do have the past to guide us with an average, along with the knowledge that *investing is where your savings can multiply.*

---

[5] B. Carlson, "Deconstructing 10, 20 & 30 Year Stock Market Returns," A Wealth of Common Sense, February 9, 2023, https://awealthofcommonsense.com/2023/02/deconstructing-10-20-30-year-stock-market-returns/

[6] John Egan, "What Average Rate of Return on 401(k) Can You Expect?" Time stamped, Nov. 30, 2023, https://time.com/personal-finance/article/average-return-rate-on-401k/

Many of you will choose to avoid the stock market altogether and will invest in other ventures such as real estate or collectibles, or lower risk CDs or Treasury notes, or numerous other ideas.

As the stock market is far and away the most popular place where investors have put their money, the reasonable 7.5% number will be the basis for our projections.

Another key factor to investment growth is **compounding.** It's a very important term to understand, and a crucial stimulus in the performance and more rapid acceleration of an investment portfolio.

**Compounding** means earning a rate of return on your investments *as well as growth already earned on top of those investments.* For instance, if you had a $100 investment and earned 7.5% on it (or $7.50) for the year, you would then have $107.50. The following year if you earned that same 7.5%, it would compound on top of the $107.50 total, adding $8.06 for a total of $115.56. The following year, whatever rate you earned would compound on top of the $115.56. This carries on throughout your investing timespan and becomes equivalent to a snowball rolling downhill at an accelerating rate, potentially multiplying numerous times depending on how long you invest.

The key to this concept is that you *must* leave your annual growth in your portfolio so that it can earn you additional interest on top of your invested money! **Compounding is relied upon by investors to create wealth!**

What will your 'final score' be at the end of your career? Your pot of gold will ultimately hold an amount that is reliant on numerous factors. More information on investing will be provided in later chapters.

Coming up in the next chapter, we will review income from a unique angle.

### *Chapter 4 Summary:*

-7.5% annual growth will be used as our baseline for projecting future growth of your savings and investments.

-You will be free to invest in whatever you like; stock market growth is highlighted due to popularity and history of 10% annual growth rate.

-Investing is time-proven as a successful method for wealth creation.

-Compounding is an important finance term meaning growth on top of already earned growth, which helps to accelerate wealth building.

-While investing has created most of the wealth in America, there is no guarantee of level of success or future amount.

# Chapter 5:
# Perspective

*"Is the glass half full, or half empty?"*

You may find this chapter to be eye opening. Let's discuss a random annual income for a moment, picking an easy round number of $12,000 annually, or $1,000 monthly (possibly representing someone working part time or who has a small business).

Someone earning near that amount may feel self-conscious in discussing their income level. Let's consider the example from another perspective...

For instance, would you be surprised to learn that there are billions (not a misprint) of people on earth who would trade places with the $1,000 per month earner *in an instant?*

Consider these head-turning numbers with respect to our world population:

About **80%** of humanity lives on the equivalent of $10 a day or less, (about $300 per month, or $3,650 per year).[7]

Wow, isn't that a staggering and mind-numbing statistic? And as surprising as it may be to learn about the scope of our world poverty situation, there is another state of poverty that is even more shocking. It's called '*absolute poverty*'. The definition of *absolute poverty* is reserved for people on earth *living on less than $2.15 a day, or about $785 per year.*[8]

---

[7] The World Bank, "Understanding Poverty", November 9, 2023, https://pip.worldbank.org/home

[8] The World Bank, "Understanding Poverty", November 9, 2023, https://pip.worldbank.org/home

You may want to sit down before learning how many people on your planet are estimated to live in the category of absolute poverty. Seated or at least out of harm's way? About 700 million live in that extreme condition. That's nearly one out of every ten people on earth!

Circling back to the example of someone earning around $1,000 a month or any other amount that is classified as poor in America, there are **billions and billions** of people who envy your wealth and would trade places to have your opportunity today, sight unseen, no test drive, no further questions asked!

Perspective is everything. While the $1,000 per month earner may be envious of 'the rich', *those 5 to 6 billion fellow humans in the world poverty classification consider a person earning $1,000 to also be wealthy, beyond their wildest dreams.*

If you are living in an industrialized nation, *you* happen to be living in an opportune place and time, with abundant opportunity, and you are about to learn how *you* can create savings and have your very own growing treasure chest of investments that can lead you to wealth in *your* brighter future!

You may not be convinced that you'll be able to find savings yet, as many of you probably feel that you already watch every dollar spent like a hawk. You will find much to consider before you have finished this book! Soon you will be able to envision your very own growing chest of treasure.

### The very same goes for those of you on a disability income.

These investment ideas have a special place for you. Do you feel 'stuck' living on a fixed disability income? Why shouldn't you be able to save and become an investor??? You also have access to and can improve your future and quality of life! Don't put this book down, it can change your circumstances for the better. Your choices can make a difference in your future!

---

If you're currently struggling just to make ends meet, I hope this chapter has provided a different perspective that can allow you to be grateful and excited for your coming opportunity.

## *Chapter 5 Summary:*

*-Regardless of current income, we are fortunate if we live in an industrialized nation, and there are billions of people on earth who would trade places to have the opportunity that we have here.*

*-All earners, even those on disability, can improve their lives by using this method.*

# Chapter 6:
# Highly Skilled At Spending

*"Expenses are everywhere!"*

One could substitute the word 'consumer' with 'money.' Where consumption is concerned, money is spent. Humans consume voraciously... Energy, food, entertainment, merchandise, services, and information all have a cost.

Do you find enjoyment in the numerous goods and services that you are purchasing today? Are you having fun in your life? **Then your retirement fund should be absolutely crucial.** Why? Imagine the feeling of having the wonderful things you love all your working life, but then not being able to afford them when you retire.

That scenario may lead to a not-so-fun decision: Retire and give the fun stuff up or keep working indefinitely. This book's method is intended to help eliminate having to make that decision.

You may recall from your school days Maslow's basic hierarchy of needs which suggests that we all inherently seek SECURITY for ourselves and our families. Yet many of us don't have enough money for the next unplanned expense that arises.

Did you know that 49% of Americans would not be able to cover a $400 emergency expense today?[9] We are aware that the next mushroom cloud is waiting for us around the next corner, however our current income, spending habits and perceived needs are keeping close to half of us from being able to afford that unplanned expense.

---

[9] Jack Flynn, "20 + Shocking American Savings Statistics (2023): Average Personal Savings Accounts, Demographics, and Facts," Zippia.com, Feb 16, 2023, https://www.zippia.com/advice/american-savings-statistics/

Let's journey together for a moment inside that mysterious locale in our brains where our desire for success resides. We are, of course, talking about the anterior cingulate cortex (attention area) and the dorsolateral prefrontal cortex (cognitive control area), which are the main neural circuits related to regulation of motivation.[10]

All right, switching back to English now, while human beings are fascinating, complex creatures, and are capable of incredible feats of innovation, we cannot get away from the fact that we are nonetheless imperfect.... We regularly witness as human behavior defies logic. Examples you may be able to identify with: "What happens if I touch this?" "I don't need the instructions." "Hold my beer and watch this."

Similar irrationalities can appear during decision making involving our money. Case in point: Without a second thought about their current woeful finances, a couple agrees, "Let's go out to eat tonight!" *YOLO and ya gotta enjoy it, right?* Who can argue with that?

What about car shopping? (Don't get you started, right?) Another couple carefully nails down their budget before going to the dealership or online. "$300 is our maximum monthly payment, agreed?! Good! Now let's have a look."

And it's not long before they are cruising around town showing off their shiny new fire red missile on wheels with a hot tub in the trunk, and a big spoiler to keep them from violating controlled airspace.

The payment was *$575 a month...* But somehow it was easy to justify; *"The bank said we could afford it!"* And when the payments begin, the couple immediately experiences a familiar, uneasy pain as they search for ways to survive their decision.

Some choices come with added, unexpected surprises. For instance, the elevated auto insurance premium might not have been

---

[10] Sung-Il Kim, "Neuroscientific Model of Motivational Process," National Institute of Health, Mar. 4, 2013, https://www.ncbi.nlm.nih.gov/pmc/articles/PMC3586760/

considered for the vehicle upgrade. "Double whammy!" Then, further salt is soon poured in the wound as they register their vehicle and pay the sizable tag fee with their state. Game, set, and match from one decision!!!

When we established the habit of purchasing, without realizing it, we created a barrier to saving. Many of us have become so talented at spending that not only is our bank account empty, but we also have debt on top! It's high time to add that missing skill and work on righting our futures.

While a lower level of earnings can be an obstacle to saving money, there are plenty of examples of low and modest-wage earners who *have* devoted a portion of their pay to savings/investments and have become wealthy.

There are also countless instances of middle- and upper-class earners who have saved *nothing*. There is a term for this group. 'High Earners, Not Rich Yet (HENRYs) is a term to describe people who earn high incomes, usually between $250,000 to $500,000, but have not saved or invested enough to be considered rich. Most of HENRY's incomes are consumed by consumer spending, educational costs, and housing.'[11] This proves a point; Income is not the only ingredient in the recipe for wealth creation.

For instance, consider that if you began putting just $20 per month into an investment account, starting when you're 20 years old, there could be a projected **$68,787** waiting in the bank for you when you are 60. That's about seven times the amount that you put in! For just $20 bucks a month... Who can't do that???... Sounds so easy, doesn't it??

Well, it's not! One analysis of the number of people who will be able to retire at 65 found that only 18 percent of families aged 25-34

---

[11] Will Kenton, "High Earners, Not Rich Yet, (HENRYs) Definition," Investopedia, December 8, 2022, https://www.investopedia.com/terms/h/high-earners-not-yet-rich-henrys.asp#:~:text=High%20Earners%2C%20Not%20Rich%20Yet%20(HENRYs)%20is%20a%20term,%2C%20educational%20costs%2C%20and%20housing.

use an IRA or Keogh plan, and just 36 percent of families aged 55-64 use one.[12]  Close to two thirds of people nearing retirement age may not have a retirement fund!

We know that we should plan and save for our coming days *at some point…*.  But often, '*some point*' arrives too late.  Time slips away and suddenly the realization hits home that retirement has snuck up on us and is just a few years away.  The idea of saving ended up on a backburner, behind all the other fun and noise that got in the way.

If an 'easier' option could be the solution to your saving difficulties, your level of excitement should be high as you turn the pages in this book.  Maybe you're wondering if a method that you can actually tolerate is around the corner. *Good news! You won't have to do things that you can't stick with to save here!*

Today if you have **no** money in the bank, **no** retirement savings, and there is **no** change to your income, tomorrow you can start saving for that retirement without even noticing it.  It could almost seem like magic.

As in our earlier example, finding and investing as little as $35 per month by updating a phone plan could make a substantial impact, and that can be just the tip of your iceberg!  Try adding a zero to the $35 figure, *and more.*  You can build as big a nest egg as *you* are comfortable with, and you'll be at the controls to virtually name your prize!

If your bank account is currently idling with little to no savings, this book's premise provides a new avenue to help you step on the accelerator and get going….  Even if you happen to have a savings or retirement fund, the opportunities you will find here can help you build a bigger treasure chest.

---

[12] https://www.cnbc.com/2019/03/12/most-americans-arent-saving-enough-to-retire-by-age-65.html

Keep in mind the investment and savings formula being promoted here is manageable. Allow yourself some hope as you learn and incorporate a method that doesn't hurt as you find and create new wealth and a brighter future.

If you happen to be highly skilled at spending, look forward to righting your ship by finding and packing your new savings away as planned. There is nothing wrong with becoming more aware and frugal with respect to your expenses. A new you along with new savings will be a *force for success*.

### *Chapter 6 Summary:*

*-In order to continue to enjoy life and its pleasures, retirees will need money. If there is no money saved, either those pleasures will have to go away, or retiring will need to be postponed, even cancelled.*

*-We are highly skilled at spending and need a method to also allow and ensure saving.*

*-Even small amounts saved regularly can become substantial over time.*

*-This method can change or improve your financial future whether you are currently saving or not.*

# Chapter 7:
# If You Already Have Savings

*"Maximize what you've got."*

If you're fortunate enough to already have a savings account balance, you might be holding a nice head start! You may be among a sizable sub-group of people who are saving *but not yet investing.*

You've probably thought about what *investing* your current savings might do to jumpstart your future. Below, you will find a table with various rounded savings amounts, as well as estimates of what those savings could be worth to you in the future if you were to put them to work for you now.

If you do consider investing the amount in your bank account, ensure you keep enough in savings to cover an unplanned visit from any surprise you can dream up. Then, feel free to invest the rest! Accelerated growth becomes possible for you.

In the tables below find the closest number to your current amount of savings that you wish to place in investments. Then scroll down to the closest number of years you believe you'll continue to work until retirement.

You'll be exposed to what your current savings could realize at a projected 7.5% annual growth rate. You may find that you're leaving a sizable hunk of your potential out of your future by not investing a percentage of your current savings! Have a look. If you have:


$1,000 to invest @ 7.5%:

Value in 10 years: $2,061

Value in 20 years: $4,248

Value in 30 years: $8,755

Value in 40 years: $18,044

You are reading correctly: Just $1,000 invested and left alone at a 7.5% average growth rate for 40 years has the potential to become nearly $20,000!

$2,500 to invest @ 7.5%:

    Value in 10 years: $5,153

    Value in 20 years: $10,620

    Value in 30 years: $21,887

    Value in 40 years: $45,111

$5,000 to invest @ 7.5%:

    Value in 10 years: $10,305

    Value in 20 years: $21,239

    Value in 30 years: $43,775

    Value in 40 years: $90,221

$10,000 to invest @ 7.5%:

    Value in 10 years: $20,610

    Value in 20 years: $42,479

    Value in 30 years: $87,550

    Value in 40 years: $180,442

$25,000 to invest @ 7.5%:

    Value in 10 years: $51,526

    Value in 20 years: $106,196

Value in 30 years: $218,874

Value in 40 years: $451,106

$50,000 to invest @ 7.5%:

Value in 10 years: $103,052

Value in 20 years: $212,393

Value in 30 years: $437,748

Value in 40 years: $902,212

$100,000 to invest @ 7.5%:

Value in 10 years: $206,103

Value in 20 years: $424,785

Value in 30 years: $875,496

Value in 40 years: $1,804,424

Some of you may be pleasantly surprised to learn that you already have a potential source of great wealth sitting in your savings bank! It's your call, decide if you want to invest your savings and get them working for you. You can synergize by adding this amount to the new savings you'll soon be finding.

If you have some savings packed away, take your estimated future value from the tables above and keep it in your back pocket until we get to the savings exercise. You will have the option to add this number to your new money saved for greater potential wealth at your retirement!

### Chapter 7 Summary:

*-By investing savings you currently have, you may be able to multiply your wealth potential.*

# Chapter 8:
# Monthly Bills.  How Did We Get Here?

*"Too talented at spending."*

Most of the way through our wondrous adventure of growing up, everything we consume is 'on the house,' no charge!  It all happens in the background of the carefree wonder years.

At some point in our early adulthood, many of us will move out of our childhood home, either by choice or by force.  We then begin that exciting journey of *freedom*, of being our own bosses and learning from our unsupervised decisions.  We might join with friends to rent an apartment, or we go-it alone.  That's when many of us get our introduction to that thing that was always in the hazy background; ***Bills!!***

Rent, heat, A/C, Water, TV, Internet, Gas, on and on the list goes.  Do you remember the first bill you received?  "It can't cost that much just to heat the house!"  (Then your subconscious stirs, '*Ah,* that's why I got yelled at when I left the lights on.  Or didn't close the door.  Or ran the water for 10 minutes before showering.')

Food was *free* when we were kids!  Going to the restaurant lost that carefree feeling as we began noticing a new column on the menu: the price!  It was a time of awakening as our feelings toward our parents may have migrated more toward the side of gratitude.  The realization of the sacrifices they made for us began to sink in.

It became *our turn* to learn how to take care of matters, and our parents and guardians were no doubt getting a kick out of it.  They also felt pride as they watched us grow and learn, even if we were a little clueless and 'a lot broke' at times.

Paying the bills took us into a new and uncertain world, a black hole that vacuumed our cash away, leaving us to survey the rubble in the aftermath of each month.

When signing up to get utilities such as water, gas and power turned on, there was no negotiation. We provided our vital info, they checked our credit, and maybe we paid a security deposit. Then we thanked them before hanging up!

We may have used those utilities abundantly, without considering the cost of consumption. (Therein may lie opportunities that we will review soon).

For many of our other monthly bills, we had decisions to make. For instance, who knew there were so many choices for ordering TV service? When you first called, the cable or satellite basic service might have started at just $59.95 a month.

Us: "Yeah, I can afford that, sign me up!" There was a negotiation that ensued.

Them: "Sure, which channel package would you like? In your 200-channel package, it doesn't include..." (here's where you learn that the 200-channel package offers about six that you would actually watch).

Us: "What's the next level?"

Them: "The 300-channel package includes shows like Real Housewives of Mt. Everest, and Potty Wars."

Us: "Um, I need them. How much is that?"

Them: "That'll be another $29.99."

Us: "Thirty bucks? Let's do it."

Them: "Do you like movies? Miniseries?"

Us: "Well, sure."

Them: "Did you know that Moo-v-flixx is now airing 'Killed to Death'? Would you like access to that?"

Us: "Woah, I have to have that." …. Bang, add $15.

Them: "How many TV's do you have? 4? They each need control boxes."

Us: "What's a control box?" Cha ching, ching, ching, ching! $15 bucks per month each, $60 more.

By now, you are getting to the point of just wanting this process over with. But they keep going.

Them: "Do you like sports? What's your favorite team? You can watch EVERY GAME of the year!!!"

Us: "Does that include the Axe Throwing Network? We need that." Ching, ching!

Them: "Almost done." You can faintly hear the calculator clicking away at a quick pace on the other end, then a brief pause. "All right, *including taxes and fees...*" Suddenly your $59.99 starting number has ballooned to $179.65 per month...

And you do it. You need to enjoy your new 250 inch 10-billion-pixel flat screen (that you may have just financed adding another new bill) to the fullest! And we haven't even begun to discuss how many streaming services you might subscribe to!

It's a similar negotiation and result for many of the other goods and services we want or need. We can be highly talented at spending money. Unless trained as an accountant, we might not fully comprehend the effect on our budget as we purchase these items.

Being a consumer can be an infinite game of temptation vs. ability to pay, and paying the monthly bills can be a relentless game of survival with seemingly no victory or end as we wait for the next round's bell to ring. How we perform in the rounds yet to come is dependent on our financial shape. And perhaps we made some miscalculations along the way, placing ourselves in perilous financial waters...

The mounting sum of our monthly obligations puts many of us on a crash course toward that first month when we decide we can't pay off a bill or our credit card.  We might even start paying bills *with* that card.  It's the beginning of our relationship with overspending and **debt.**  We then have a new, unwelcome manager in control of our financial affairs.

If you find yourself among this group, you have plenty of company.  A survey found that 49% of Americans depend on credit cards to cover essential living expenses.[13]

Unfortunately, becoming a member of the borrowing club pushes the important task of securing our future further out of the picture.  There is nothing to save.  And for many, that grim fact may never change.

### *Chapter 8 Summary:*

*-We typically learn about bill paying the hard way as we become adults.*

*-We are not all accounting experts and may not have full control of our budgets, or what we spend or why.*

*-A large percentage spend more than their earnings, leading to debt woes.*

*-Overspending is an added barrier between us and saving.*

---

[13] Gabrielle Olya, "Jaw-Dropping Stats About the State of Debt in America," Yahoo.com, January 30, 2023 www.yahoo.com/now/jaw-dropping-stats-state-credit-130022967.html

# Chapter 9:
# The Elephant In The Bills

*"We're broke!"*

A high percentage of consumers whose obligations hit 'tilt' need to resort to credit to finance their bills and purchases. Whether by necessity or in the pursuit of excitement, using credit can become an easy escape that carries with it a draining commitment.

Credit cards are a way of life in our society, and they are not always used wisely. If you are in debt, there's a lurking problem behind every financial decision and transaction you make. Every month when you pick up your stack of bills, it may feel as if there is an elephant laying on them. Until your debts are fully paid, that weight remains.

"Many find themselves slipping deeper in debt, some of it at a very high and punishing interest rate. Our entire country is in the habit of using credit and debt to pay for goods and services. American households carry a total of $17 trillion in debt as of the first quarter of 2023, ...and the average credit card balance as of Q3, 2022 is $5,910."[14]

Credit and debt payments further stifle any chance to save. Paying interest is equivalent to having another bill on top of the goods and services already being paid for.

Interest payments reduce both our spending power and the ability to cover our expenses. Does that sound interchangeable with another financial term? *Inflation* has a similar effect. Living a financed life,

---

[14] Jack Caporal, "Average American Household Debt in 2023," Facts and Figures, Motley Fool, August 17, 2023, https://www.fool.com/the-ascent/research/average-household-debt/

coupled with inflation doubles the negative forces against the value of your dollar.

The debt elephant welcomes a relationship with us, making credit readily available. If we begin to build a balance, repaying our obligations is made to seem quite simple! Those cards magically allow you the enticing choice to pay just a tiny minimum amount back each month. "I just charged $3,000 dollars and my monthly payment is only $30! How lucky is that?! This is awesome, let's go buy something else!!"

But we instinctively know when we're paying the monthly minimum that something is not right. And our instincts would be correct! We could be paying that $30 in near-perpetuity.

The minimum payment is a time extension that makes every month feel like Deja Vu. If you're already struggling to make ends meet, the minimum is helpful in covering the month's other bills. But, per our intuition, here are a couple of harsh realities on why it can seem like we make minimum payments forever: "In part, that's because the minimum is usually so low that it just barely exceeds the interest charges that accrue each month on your balance. When you're just paying the minimum, it could take years — in some cases, decades — to pay off your full balance."[15]

Do you recall our chapter discussing the benefits of compounding interest? This time, it's the credit card companies that are benefiting from compounding, received from you. "Paying only the minimum keeps you in debt longer, costs you money in interest and could hurt your credit score."[16] For contrast, saving $30 monthly can pack your account full of treasure, rather than giving away $30 in interest.

---

[15] Claire Tsosie, "How Credit Card Companies Calculate Minimum Payments," Nerd Wallet, November 28, 2022, https://www.nerdwallet.com/article/credit-cards/credit-card-issuer-minimum-payment

[16] Claire Tsosie, "What Happens if I Make Only the Minimum Payment on my Credit Card?" Nerd Wallet, July 14, 2021, https://www.nerdwallet.com/article/credit-cards/minimum-payment-credit-card

When you are paying bills, if interest is paid in any of them, they should be your least favorite, because they have NEGATIVE VALUE to you. It is in your very best *interest* (appropriate!) that you first eliminate this credit anchor from your life.

So, let's pick a number and suggest someone with credit card debt of $5,000 uncovers opportunities in this book that increase their cash on hand by a total of $200 per month, or $2,400 annually. *If they are patient and don't invest that newly found money just yet, and rather send it toward paying off their card balance(s)they can ultimately have a bigger chest of treasure in their investment account.*

Meticulously and purposely pay off as much of your credit card and other debt as possible. You can be debt free in less than two years when you combine the $30 minimum payment and the $200 toward payoff. Talk about changing your life! Eliminating interest payments is when you take charge of your financial future and income, rather than the debt elephant weighing in on *your* life's direction.

Once you've paid your credit card balance off completely, transfer that $230 into your investment account every month. See the sizable estimates below:

10-year projected savings: $40,373

20-year projected savings: $123,580

30-year projected savings: $295,073

40-year projected savings: $648,525

Woah…

If you don't take advantage of this opportunity, the paunchy pachyderm will continue to weigh you down and will siphon your minimum payments for many years to come, until you may have paid double, triple or more for your charges! That would cause the potential returns you see above to disappear.

Investments are another source of income for you, equivalent to having a pay raise or a second job! *Rather than paying interest, better to be the one who earns it!!!!!!* (ran out of exclamation points).

If you are in debt today, I hope you are coming to the logical conclusion that, before you can begin to build your retirement fortune, you'll need to eliminate your toxic interest payments. The weight of the debt elephant is sapping your earnings strength and keeping you from the prize! Your new savings dollars can rescue you from your debt earlier than planned.

Agree to never borrow money or use credit cards again unless you can pay for them *entirely* that month! My friends, that practice will go very far in ensuring your happier and more secure future.

## *Chapter 9 Summary:*

*-Credit cards and debt make it extremely difficult to save for our future.*

*-Minimum payments are full of interest and devoid of principle.*

*-Paying interest is equivalent to having another bill.*

*-As you create your savings using this book, direct them toward paying off your debt before using them for investing. This simple strategy will create the opportunity for greater wealth.*

# Chapter 10:
## Surprise!  The Best Monthly Bill!

*"A simple idea for having the things you desire."*

If one chapter can have more impact on your future than the rest, this could be it.  Beginning with pre-school and every step of the way through completing our highest level of education, we are taught many subjects that prepare us for adult life.

It's safe to say that our schooling doesn't cover every important aspect of what we need to know and might miss the mark on some important life concepts.  Topics such as managing a successful marriage… creating a budget… proper child rearing… doing the right thing… investing and planning for retirement… are often not taught.  <u>Perhaps until today, until this moment, some of you have never thought of **your future as one of the best and most important 'monthly bills' you will pay in your lifetime.**</u>

It seems counter-intuitive; "Another bill???"  **The GREAT NEWS to remember is that you are *paying yourself.*  While it feels like another obligation, *it's still yours!*  This is the one bill that you should pay with a big smile on your face!  Your net worth grows each time you pay it!  As investments, your monthly contributions can multiply!**

For those of you who are not able to save yet, (actually, for everyone), this chapter emphasizes the importance of taking care of your future.  With forward thinking and management of the years ahead of us as an obligation or **monthly bill,** it becomes a commonsense *requirement* to devote a portion of our earnings (i.e. your about-to-be newfound savings) to your future.

Many of your friends, co-workers and acquaintances are already in on this secret as they contribute to their 401k's or another investment type.  This is how you will turn your *unknown* future into a more *certain* time!

What do you expect out of your retirement? Do you want more excitement? How about just being able to maintain your current lifestyle? If either of the above sounds appealing, then you need to pay your retirement 'bill'! Building a retirement should be a mandatory concept for everyone and an idea that every person expects to begin contributing to when they first start earning money.

With our ever-increasing lifespan, for the average person who retires at age 65, it's possible to live another 30 years, *plus*. Our retirement years can approach one-third of our total lifespan. It's imperative that we're able to enjoy that time and live contented lifestyles for that timeframe!

Take a moment and consider the bills you're paying today. Which among them is more important than ensuring a secure tomorrow and a retirement that allows you to afford the things you want? Using your new savings, happily add this one payment to the items for which you are currently paying.

Do you use autopay on some or all your current monthly bills? If so, then this concept is going to be *easy* for you! That's exactly how you'll save and invest for your future. You'll have your future on autopilot!

Pop Quiz! What happens to someone who doesn't pay their bills? That's correct, they lose the right to have what they originally agreed to pay for. Using that same thinking, if someone does not pay toward their retirement, what happens to that 'right' when the time arrives?

**"Treat your retirement like it's a bill", and you will have a retirement."** This is basic and yet important…

Let's discuss Social Security for a moment. If you happen to be contributing FICA payroll tax and earning Social Security credits, please check your Social Security estimated payment amount for retirement. What is your current projected amount? Now, calculate how much you currently spend each month. You will probably see a gap, confirming that by itself, the amount of monthly Social Security income you receive at retirement cannot comfortably support a future full of all the things you love, the fun, the travel, leisure, and luxury. You need *more*.

Focus on investing in your own retirement fund with the idea of combining this with your Social Security. The savings exercise will allow you the opportunity to customize your projected amount in your treasure chest!

In the all-important chapters that create your savings, take a closer look at the things that you pay for each month and ask yourself if they outrank your future. Determine what can be altered or revised without pain to help you begin securing your retirement. Be confident that you can find a handful of expenses to reduce that don't hurt or upstage the importance of your cozy future!

Once you've finished choosing those savings opportunities, we'll then move you right into transferring and investing that money in the same manner you pay your bills.

Pop Quiz #2: Except for your home, can you name any of your monthly expenses that can grow in value for you? While bills consume your money, you're correct again, your *retirement bill* is an exception that can grow for *you!*

*Saving and investing in your retirement should rank among the most important bills that you will EVER pay.*

Save. Invest. Pay that 'bill.' <u>It will become a habit</u>. When the magical day arrives and it's time for you to 'hang up your spikes,' having a waiting portfolio will make the conversation around the house a bit more invigorating than if you haven't prepared for it.

Below are exciting questions to be able to ponder upon your retirement:

'Ready to celebrate with a vacation?'

'Should I remodel?'

'How many trips do we want to take each year?'

'Where should we look for a 2$^{nd}$ home?'

'What kind of boat do I want?'

'What charity should we donate to?'

'How can we best help our church?'

'How much money do we want to leave for our children?'

Those can be fun questions. They originate from the hearts and minds of people who have built wealth for their retirement.

Compare them to these not so thrilling questions:

'Am I going to need to work forever?'

'I wonder if we'll be able to afford a vacation sometime?'

'Will Social Security cover my expenses, or will I need to keep working?'

'Do you think anyone will leave us money?'

'I wonder if our kids will take care of us?'

The latter group is a list of questions that I hope you won't be asking someday, and if you haven't begun saving already, *the action you're taking now, today,* and every dollar that you save and invest will help to improve your odds of being the owner of the *good* kind of retirement questions. And answers!

## *Chapter 10 Summary:*

*-Think of your retirement as another bill you must pay. The good news is you are paying yourself, it's still yours!*

*-Social Security monthly payments are a means of survival and probably won't provide for the lifestyle you're accustomed to.*

*-By devoting savings toward your future, you increase your chances of being able to ask the good kind of questions!*

# Chapter 11:
# Keep It Fun

*"Enjoy the ride."*

You will soon debut your new financial trajectory and future by becoming a saver and an investor. It's a great move on your part and you know it! But *why* have you decided on this course of action? Because you know it's the right thing to do? Because you're tired of not having money available? While you're taking this positive action, remember to celebrate some exciting times your new funds are creating!

Emphasize some goals or desires in life that you've dreamt about. Have you envisioned a particular vacation? Have you hoped you could help your children avoid the debt they'll incur as they pursue their higher education goals? Has there been a mountain home in your dreams?

As you analyze each of the upcoming money saving opportunities that you *will* find, consider making a fun game out of it! Maybe $10k saved in one area is going toward that vacation to Italy that you'll take. Perhaps $50k saved in another is the college tuition gift that you've always dreamed of surprising your child with. What if the next $100k you'll save is going toward your dream cabin in the Carolinas or Montana? (Some of you are looking at these 'dreams' with doubt, thinking they're inflated beyond your level. Start the process, and you'll become convinced and more engaged at what is possible...)

Cut out a picture of the Coliseum in Rome and tape it onto your fridge or pin it to your corkboard. Add a clip of a cap and gown for your son/daughter with their imaginary college diploma(s) in their hand. Then find a mountain landscape photo that takes your breath away. Your refrigerator can become a motivator and an inspiration every time you open it!

Consider adding tangible individual goals to your determination in your investing efforts. And be SURE to reward yourself along the way. Celebrate each milestone and achievement with a night out or a quick getaway. You earned it!

Every time you check your soon-to-be growing account balance, you might do it with more excitement and purpose. Keep investing fun as you monitor your progress toward your goals!

## *Chapter 11 Summary:*

*-Add the ideas you dream about to your investing efforts. You are now creating the opportunity to make them come true!*

*-Be sure to celebrate milestones along the road as you fill your treasure chest!*

# Chapter 12:
# Things You Might Want To Spend More Money On

*"Look at things from another angle."*

*WHAT???* This chapter goes 180 degrees against the idea of saving money! Well, we don't want anyone going overboard with our savings concept. There are certain things in life that you might want to spend *more* money on and avoid when on sale. Gas station sushi comes to mind....

Would you take advantage of a going-out-of-business sale at a tattoo parlor? Cheap space shuttle ride? Half-off surgery? *(If you order before midnight tonight, we'll include a second vasectomy at no additional cost!)* Slightly irregular parachutes!!!??? Clearance sale on mountain climbing ropes!!?? Not for me, no thank you....

In general, most of the things we pay for can be negotiated or purchased at a discount to save you money without jeopardizing your life or lifestyle, but there are always things that you should consider spending top dollar on.

**What Else Should I Pay More For?**

If you don't have life insurance now, and if you provide for your family or a dependent or spouse, you need it! Especially if you're about to build your retirement empire. If you plan to have a million dollars in your family's retirement fund when you're 59 ½, the only way to *guarantee* that to happen is to also insure your life as you save toward your goal.

It may be hard to visualize spending money in the event of your own death. "All I've ever known is being alive, what could go wrong?" you might ask. Do you need someone to start a list for you? Yes, those chances are low, but do you want to risk your family living in need without you?

Let's say that as you go through the savings exercise, you identify $200 in new monthly savings. If you have dependents and don't have life insurance yet, you might want to consider it. You can take whatever portion of that $200 per month that will comfortably pay for a policy that covers your worst-case scenario. That's what insurance is designed for, and it means the people who count on you are safe and secure because of YOU and your decisions.

Do you have an umbrella policy? Your auto insurance policy typically has a $300,000 coverage limit. If you're ever sued for an auto accident, for instance, and if the plaintiff attempts to collect damages greater than the coverage limits of your auto insurance, your assets could be vulnerable, (aside from your home and auto). If you are or plan to become worth an amount well above that $300,000 limit, a million-dollar umbrella policy could be a good idea to consider.

Let's keep going on the 'what should you pay more for' idea. If you have mortgaged your home, there is a simple way to save a massive amount of money. (To do this, you must be in a good financial situation already, and you should also be maxing out your retirement savings).

Anyone who has the means to double their mortgage payment, or even make just one extra payment per year will create the ability to eliminate this massive loan and interest paid much earlier than planned. Getting out of debt is a primary key to having wealth.

All your extra payments go straight toward paying off the principal balance, saving you the interest that would have been charged. This could be worth tens to hundreds of thousands in interest charges, depending on your home value...

How about tipping? Consider being more generous with the people who serve your food and beverage, wash or park your car, clean your hotel room, load your bags, golf clubs, skis, etc.

If you want to see someone's eyes light up with joy due to a small consideration, try giving a $10 tip to the 15-year-old teenager who serves you at the ice cream stand. Tell them you appreciated their attentiveness or professionalism. It's a priceless feeling to make someone's day! Money is nothing without happiness. It's ok to share if you can afford it, and the feeling is rewarding.

Another topic: Do you wake up sometimes wondering if your bank account is still safe or if your laptop will greet you with 'Good morning sucker!' as you start the day? Can your identity and possessions get stolen and be in someone else's name? Identity protection and cybersecurity might be good things to spend money on, and you'll sleep better. Look into it if you don't already have this coverage, it can be as little as $10 per month.

Speaking of cybersecurity, how about a benefit that's free? Rather than talking about spending money....let's focus on avoiding losing it! If you don't already utilize added layers of security for your bank account, credit cards and retirement account, you will want to use the 'double authentication' option.

By picking this option, with every attempt you make to login, you'll get a text or email to verify it's you. Even if someone was able to steal your password, they can't get entry into your account without double authentication.

Always keep your eyes open for additional savings, but don't go overboard. Take care of your business by spending *more* money where it makes sense!

### *Chapter 12 Summary:*

*-While it's important to be cost conscious, there are times when spending more money makes sense.*

*-Take care of your family's future with insurance. Protect your important accounts with added security.*

# Chapter 13:
# How To Employ The Savings Worksheet

*"Preparation is the key to success!"*

We're getting close to the reason you picked up this book. In the very next chapter, you'll be considering dozens and dozens of savings opportunities.

This chapter includes a walk-through exercise explaining how to fill out the SAVINGS WORKSHEET you'll use as you go through the next chapter! Please review and ensure you understand how to use the worksheet, which will help to make certain the savings exercise is a memorable moment for you.

At the end of this chapter, you'll find your own blank SAVINGS WORKSHEET to write your ideas and totals on. Note, there is an extra in Appendix A should you need it. If you would prefer to print a copy or use our online SAVINGS WORKSHEET, you can do so by visiting our website at findyourhiddentreasurechest.com.

Let's review the SAMPLE SAVINGS WORKSHEET as it is filled out from top to bottom below. The first two lines are self-explanatory, number of years to retirement, and your goal/amount you would like to have when you retire.

Below the first two lines, there are five columns. The first column, OPPORTUNITY AND NOTES is where you will annotate each savings idea you are interested in.

The next column is where you will input the PROJ MO SAVINGS, or projected monthly savings of the opportunity.

Next is TOT PROJ MO SVGS, or total projected monthly savings. You will add each of the PROJ MO SAVINGS into this column.

You will write the projected long-term investment savings for the opportunity in the PROJ LT SAVINGS column.

In the final column, TOT PROJ LT SVGS, or total projected long-term savings, you'll add and input each of the PROJ LT SAVINGS. This is the overall projection for your savings!

Let's do a walk-through exercise. We'll say that the list in our exercise belongs to a nice lady named Carly. Carly is 27 years old, has one dollar in her bank as of today, and she has selected 40 years as her target timeframe, which would have her retiring at around age 67. She is going to attempt to customize her future and has chosen a goal of having one million dollars in her account upon her retirement. She writes these numbers at the top of her worksheet.

**SAVINGS WORKSHEET (SAMPLE)**

PROJECTED NUMBER OF YEARS TO RETIREMENT ____40____

RETIREMENT GOAL ___$1,000,000_____

As she studies the list of savings opportunities, Carly first decides to call her mobile phone company and find a way to cut her bill by at least $15 per month. She sees that over her 40-year timeframe, she could amass a projected $42,312 at the 7 ½ percent growth estimate. She writes those numbers across the first line of her Savings Worksheet, below.

**SAVINGS WORKSHEET (SAMPLE)**

PROJECTED NUMBER OF YEARS TO RETIREMENT ____40____

RETIREMENT GOAL ____$1,000,000____

| OPPORTUNITY AND NOTES | PROJ MO SAVINGS | TOT PROJ MO SVGS | PROJ LT SAVINGS | TOT PROJ LT SVGS |
|---|---|---|---|---|
| Cell Phone | $15 | $15 | $42,312 | $42,312 |

Next, Carly considers her routine of picking up coffee on the way to work and says, "You know what, I'm stopping the coffee drive-thru today! I'll buy a nice coffee maker and a fabulous travel mug. We'll begin directing $100 savings per month into our retirement fund."

She sees that the projection for her $100 monthly savings is an incredible $281,978 over the next 40 years! She writes in the next line for the opportunity. Carly adds the two monthly savings opportunities together for a new 'TOT PROJ MO SVGS' of $115.

She writes the $281,978 projected lifetime savings below the 'PROJ LT SAVINGS' column, and she adds the 'PROJ LT SAVINGS' column numbers together for her new total in 'TOT PROJ LT SVGS' of $324,272. Her adrenaline rushes and she continues the exercise.

## SAVINGS WORKSHEET (SAMPLE)

PROJECTED NUMBER OF YEARS TO RETIREMENT _____40_____

RETIREMENT GOAL _____$1,000,000_____

| OPPORTUNITY AND NOTES | PROJ MO SAVINGS | TOT PROJ MO SVGS | PROJ LT SAVINGS | TOT PROJ LT SVGS |
|---|---|---|---|---|
| Cell Phone | $15 | $15 | $42,312 | $42,312 |
| Cut Drive Thru Coffee | 100 | 115 | 281,978 | 324.272 |

Next, she selects to save by adjusting her thermostat down or up at night, depending on the time of year, which she estimates can save her about $9 each month and $25,394 in projected savings. She continues adding her total which has now grown to $349,648.

# SAVINGS WORKSHEET (SAMPLE)

PROJECTED NUMBER OF YEARS TO RETIREMENT _____40_____

RETIREMENT GOAL _____$1,000,000_____

| OPPORTUNITY AND NOTES | PROJ MO SAVINGS | TOT PROJ MO SVGS | PROJ LT SAVINGS | TOT PROJ LT SVGS |
|---|---|---|---|---|
| Cell Phone | $15 | $15 | $42,312 | $42,312 |
| Cut Drive Thru Coffee | 100 | 115 | 281,978 | 324.272 |
| Reduce Thermostat | 9 | 124 | 25,394 | 349,648 |

Next, Carly finds that she is willing to reduce her auto insurance policy by $16 monthly by eliminating towing and rental car coverage. She does this after seeing the potential $45,132 total projected savings amount and comparing the benefit with the savings.

She also knows she can streamline her grocery shopping spending and plans to add another $20 monthly to her savings contribution.

Carly can see exactly how her progress is toward her initial goal. As she continues, she notices that when eating out, she almost always orders an appetizer. It would be simple enough to cut that out, when considering the savings potential. She estimates she eats out about twice a month. She'll plan to save and add $30 to her monthly contribution.

The next one is a big one, but not a sacrifice as Carly defines it as she attempts to customize her goal of a million dollars in her bank account. She's making the move to bagging her lunch which she justifies will also create more time for freedom during lunch hour. She sees this reduction as significant at an estimated $120 monthly saved!

She can see that she is getting closer to her goal, with her investments now projected to be worth $874,903 in 40 years! **Carly is stunned at her projection and at how little she is giving up for the life-changing number she is witnessing.**

Next, Carly finds what she thinks is a perfect option. She commits to taking care of her own dog grooming, saving an estimated $50 per month. As she adds that projected 40-year savings of $140,998, she realizes this is a big moment; When Carly adds this last idea, her total savings projection meets her overall goal of $1 million!!! Below is her completed worksheet:

**SAVINGS WORKSHEET (SAMPLE)**

| OPPORTUNITY AND NOTES | PROJ MO SAVINGS | TOT PROJ MO SVGS | PROJ LT SAVINGS | TOT PROJ LT SVGS |
|---|---|---|---|---|
| Cell Phone | $15 | $15 | $42,312 | $42,312 |
| Cut Drive Thru Coffee | 100 | 115 | 281,978 | 324.272 |
| Reduce Thermostat | 9 | 124 | 25,394 | 349,648 |
| Reduce Auto Ins Payment | 16 | 140 | 45,132 | 394,762 |
| Cut Grocery Expense | 20 | 160 | 56,410 | 451,154 |
| Cut Restaurant Exp/Appetizer | 30 | 190 | 84,606 | 535,742 |
| Bag Lunch from Now On | 120 | 310 | 338,370 | 874,093 |
| Cut Our Dog's Hair (est. $50) | 50 | 360 | 140,998 | 1,015,073 |

**AMOUNT TO TRANSFER TO INV ACCT MONTHLY: $360** *I think is realistic which projects to $1,015,073 in 40 years! I will review and try to add every year!*

Carly can't wait to begin paying her monthly 'bill' toward her future (which suddenly seems a whole lot brighter) and to get these savings headed into her new investment account. She double checks and her take home pay is unaffected.

For *your* personal worksheet at the end of this chapter, there are two suggested ways to approach your savings:

1. Customize Your Future: This was the approach Carly took. You can choose a monetary goal that you would like to see in your retirement account! You'll then work toward your goal by building the projected savings to reach said goal. What's your initial idea as a target to shoot for? $50,000 - $100,000? - $250,000? - $500,000? - $1,000,000? - $5,000,000? Don't

worry about your first attempt at your goal. You can *always* adjust it in either direction!

2. Simply find your manageable savings. You don't have to write down a goal. You can simply begin selecting savings ideas and find out what your future might look like as you move through the opportunities.

There are 60-plus money saving categories and opportunities with supporting data and research to aid with your thought process and monetary projections.

IMPORTANT: THE OPPORTUNITIES ARE IN ALPHABETICAL ORDER AND CAN VARY GREATLY IN SAVINGS POTENTIAL TO YOU. YOU'LL SEE IDEAS THAT MIGHT SEEM RIDICULOUS FOR YOU, AND THAT'S FINE, JUST KEEP MOVING!

*The monthly savings amounts are reasonable suggestions based on research but may not match your estimate. Adjust that number up or down based on what's realistic for you.*

*All the income generating projections assume that you have just $1 dollar of savings in the bank now!*

Challenge yourself to find at least three ideas to begin with. Remember that a handful of small savings will evolve into something more impactful. Turn the page for your blank worksheet, and be excited…

# SAVINGS WORKSHEET

PROJECTED NUMBER OF YEARS TO RETIREMENT _____

RETIREMENT GOAL $_____

| OPPORTUNITY AND NOTES | PROJ MO SAVINGS | TOT PROJ MO SVGS | PROJ LT SAVINGS | TOT PROJ LT SVGS |
|---|---|---|---|---|
| | | | | |
| | | | | |
| | | | | |
| | | | | |
| | | | | |
| | | | | |
| | | | | |
| | | | | |
| | | | | |
| | | | | |
| | | | | |
| | | | | |
| | | | | |
| | | | | |
| | | | | |

**TOTAL TO TRANSFER TO INV ACCT MONTHLY:** $_____

# Chapter 14:
# The Savings Opportunities
# A Through B

**Alcohol:**

Alcohol isn't first for any reason other than we are doing this alphabetically. Any paranoia is self-induced!

Let's begin with your buying habits. If you typically purchase wine by the bottle at your grocery shop, or if you're picking up your beer by the six pack, let's make sure you're not peeing some of your hard-earned money away!

What happens if you begin buying your alcohol in bulk? If you're not planning to eliminate libations from your life within the next week or two, there is serious money to be diverted right into that retirement account that has your name on it.

Wine: Let's say you are a casual wine drinker consuming about one bottle per week, or four bottles a month. You can save about 1-2 dollars per bottle when you purchase your vino by the case. That can be about $6 saved a month. That tiny amount projects to $8,916 saved when invested over 30 years at an 8% growth rate!!! Or an extra $19,348 over 40 years. Why not plan ahead and buy in bulk to have these extra riches in your pocket rather than putting them in someone else's? $6 saved and invested monthly:

10-year projected savings: $1,055

20-year projected savings: $3,228

30-year projected savings: $7,706

40-year projected savings: $16,936

It may be appropriate that the first opp is worth only $6 per month. What's important is that you identify your savings and then ensure to direct that amount into your bank, no matter how small. They will add up! With each savings idea you accept, make sure you include that amount on your worksheet!

Returning to the vino discussion, if your taste buds and palate are not too picky (in other words any wine will do) you can save even more. There are many wines available that sell by the case for less than $4 a bottle. If you're already getting the 'cheap' stuff for about $7 a bottle, look at the savings you can realize if you purchase less expensive wine by the case: If you're going through a bottle a week, you could be saving up to $12 per month. Let's round it down to $10. What does that look like when saved and invested monthly?

10-year investment savings: $1,757

20-year investment savings: $5,377

30-year investment savings: $12,838

40-year investment savings: $28,214

*Wine-ing pays off!!!*

Now, if you're averaging closer to, for instance, five bottles a week, (I know you're out there), wow, you can truly change your circumstances! If you're not already, make a small tweak and begin purchasing in bulk and/or purchase the less expensive vino at a savings of about $3 per bottle. These numbers are about to clear your foggy head:

You could be saving upwards of $60 per month, and you're now talking significance with respect to investing: Would having an extra *$75,000* dollars in your pocket in 30 years be of interest?? And, if you're able to navigate downing five bottles a week for the next *40 years*, just by reducing your cost by $3 per bottle, would you believe that you could have *close to $170,000* in your retirement fund? All you need to do is enact the change and ensure you invest your savings! $60 saved and invested monthly:

10-year projected savings: $10,534

20-year projected savings: $32,241

30-year projected savings: $76,982

40-year projected savings: $169,194

*It's like you're getting paid to drink!*

(QUICK AND IMPORTANT SIDEBAR!): Throughout the savings exercise, you will see opportunities that will surpass the $100,000 projection in investment wealth. Most are in longer retirement timeframes, but not all. Even the 10-year timeframe will see some big numbers! End sidebar.

Beer: The same savings concept goes for beer by the case. How many times have you stopped for gas, and while waiting for your tank to fill, you stepped into the beer cave and picked up a beer or two, or a six pack?

Let's look at 2 of the most popular beer brands on the market. As of this writing, they're about $5.79 a six pack. You can typically purchase a case of the same for about $19.99.

Why give more money to Mr. B or Mr. C when there's a simple way to keep it in your pocket? If you're drinking a case of beer every month, that tweak can mean a vacation, a new furniture set or A/C unit that's paid for. Even just $3 a month looks like this when invested:

10-year projected savings: $529

20-year projected savings: $1,616

30-year projected savings: $3,857

40-year projected savings: $8,477

*Turn your brew into "Wooooo"!!!*

I hope you took a moment to consider the 40-year savings on investing just $3 per month. This reinforces the 'taking care of the small leaks' concept, as well as the value of compounding your savings, no matter how small. Over that 40-year period, at an 8% growth rate, your total $1,440 investment has the potential to become almost $10,000, something of *real value!*

Run your own numbers based on your personal consumption. If you're drinking two, three or more cases of beer monthly, changing how you purchase could create a nice windfall of money in your future.

Liquor/Spirits: The concept of bulk purchase also applies for those of you who enjoy liquor or spirits. One of my favorites sells for $25.99 for a 750 ml bottle, and $44.99 for the 1.75 size. There are 250 ml more whiskey in the larger bottle compared with buying two bottles separately, and I've also saved $8 compared with buying 2!

Going through a bottle a month and making the change in size would save about $10 monthly based on the extra volume in the 1.75 liter-bottle. And what's $10 per month projected to be worth in 30 years? Over $12,000. Who wouldn't make that simple change?!?!?! $10 saved monthly:

10-year investment savings: $1,757

20-year investment savings: $5,377

30-year investment savings: $12,838

40-year investment savings: $28,214

*Turn that mash into cash! With every sip, you're busy building your fortune!!!*

Shifting gears, do you sometimes like to eliminate the stress of the day by having a little fun while out at a bar with friends?

If you prefer to sit at a bar as you order your beer, wine, or cocktail, how much could be saved by sitting at *your own bar* at home? If you're going out once a week and dropping twenty-five or fifty dollars or more on a couple of hours of fun...

What if you set up your very own cozy little bar and atmosphere at home, complete with music, TV, and your favorite libations? Invite your friends over and have that drink and watch the game sitting at home instead! Ask them to BYOB and save them some money as well!

You can purchase your own bar for as little as a couple hundred dollars and decorate it per your style, with your team colors, as a tropical paradise, or however you like it! Add a mini fridge for a couple hundred more.

You can still go out when you want but by leaving the house less frequently, you'll recoup your expense on the bar in a short time and you and your place can be the life of the party! My best friend Gary put a bar in his basement years ago and hanging out there created some of the greatest memories!

What if you moved forward with this idea and saved and directed just $50 per month from the register of the tavern into your investment account? You can surely help create a more secure future! $50 saved monthly =

10-year projected savings: $8,778

20-year projected savings: $26,869

30-year projected savings: $64,153

40-year projected savings: $140,998

*You wanna go where everybody knows your name!!!*

Don't forget: No matter how you like to unwind, have a driving rule for yourself and your friends! Hundreds of Uber rides are less expensive than just one trip to jail, court appearances, a lost job, a felony, and the risk of hurting yourself or someone else!

## Apps

How many apps do you have on your phone? What do they each cost, and do you still use them all? Many apps and games cost between $2 and $9 per month. If you're unsure, have a look at your list of apps, and if you find even one that can be sent back into cyberspace saving you $5 each month, that amount might return you much more down the road. Just $5 saved monthly:

10-year projected savings: $880

20-year projected savings: $2,691

30-year projected savings: $6,423

40-year projected savings: $14,116

*App-rehend your savings!!!*

## ATM

When you realize you need some cash, do you find yourself pulling into the next ATM you see to get your money? Do you hit 'yes' when the prompt tells you it will cost you $3 to proceed and be handed your own money? Does that hurt, even a little bit?

Try this easy life change instead; Set parameters! Whenever your pocket cash gets below $20 or $200, (whatever your 'low fuel' limit is), then take the time to pull into *your* bank's ATM for cash. You'll save on fees every month and year.

If you *invest* a little time to review your bank statements for the prior year, you'll be able to see exactly how much money you have given away needlessly to strange banks and convenience stores by not planning ahead. You'll know if this opp is worth a go. And, at those times when you *must* get money and pay the fee, withdraw as much as you can afford to so the fee is a smaller percentage of your withdrawal.

Even if you're saving just two withdrawals, or about $6 per month....

10-year projected savings: $1,055

20-year projected savings: $3,228

30-year projected savings: $7,706

40-year projected savings: $16,936

*Paying to withdraw your own money is equivalent to paying interest! Plan ahead and save so you can invest your savings and earn that interest instead!!*

### Auto Payment, Reduce or Eliminate It!

Raise your hand if you currently have no savings, *and* you have a car payment. If your hand is in the air, (and even for those who do have some money saved), there is an alternative option to that payment that could dramatically transform your coming days.

Some data: The (current) average monthly car payment for new cars is $716. The average monthly car payment for used cars is $526.[17] Let's suggest a $400 payment.

Some of us will purchase ten or more vehicles during our lifetime. We're all aware of the 'you lose money as soon as you drive it off the lot' concept, making the practice of buying used cars a generally good money saving move. And, good news, there are other ways to save money with respect to ownership of a vehicle.

---

[17] Rebecca Betterton, "Average Car Payments in 2023,", Bankrate, October 9, 2023, https://www.bankrate.com/loans/auto-loans/average-monthly-car-payment/

If you have an auto payment now, (currently, about 80% of new cars and 40% of used cars are financed)[18] how much is it?

How would you feel about trying this little tweak to change your tomorrows; Reduce your monthly car payment, take the difference, and drive it toward your future! Suddenly, instead of just a car, you would have a vehicle *and* a growing retirement account! Here's an example:

According to our online calculator, a $20,000 loan at 5% for 60 months = **$377** monthly payments.

Whereas a $15,000 loan at 5% for 60 months = **$283** monthly payments, or a savings of somewhere around $94 per month.

In the example above, the subject determined that close to $400 monthly could be afforded. Whatever your payment is, rather than devote it ALL to the car, what if you could settle on a later model, or a less expensive vehicle? Both the car *and savings* are desired, correct? A solution can be found that satisfies both needs.

With this savings opportunity, you would head back to the dealership, with the goal of trading in your vehicle for another that would have a lower payment. You choose the amount! Do you want to put $100 monthly toward your future? $200, or more?

One could decide to settle for a lower cost or higher mileage vehicle than currently owned to satisfy the savings need. One could still have a wonderful vehicle to drive as well as taking care of their needed growing future.

Let's look at directing the $94 in our example above, as well as using this strategy for all future vehicle purchases. The $94 savings is directed right into your investment account, (which we will create before you close this book) and here's the wonderful magic that can

---

[18] Chris Horymski, "Average Auto Loan Balances Grew 7.7% in 2022," April 26, 2023, Experian, https://www.experian.com/blogs/ask-experian/research/auto-loan-debt-study/

happen: $94 saved and invested monthly (as a reminder, using our projected 7.5% growth rate) =

10-year projected savings = $16,501

20-year projected savings = $50,509

30-year projected savings = $120,600

40-year projected savings = $265,060

Wow, that could be a nice chunk of money saved. If your desire is even *more money* saved to invest, what if you went 50/50 and directed $200 toward the car, (higher mileage), and $200 toward your future? Even more life changing and perhaps it's a reasonable compromise for you? $200 monthly invested =

10-year projected savings = $35,107

20-year projected savings = $107,461

30-year projected savings = $256,586

40-year projected savings = $563,938

The numbers above can be significant progress toward a retirement goal and possibly an alternate solution you can live with. What we are after is little to no sacrifice on your part. This is one idea that would help to put your desired future in place! What's a good combination for you? Even if you put just $20 of your vehicle budget monthly toward your future, you're saving!!!

Your amount will no-doubt be different from our examples above. If you want to drill this idea down further, visit our website at findyourhiddentreasurechest.com and enter a desired monthly savings amount ($100, $200 etc.) and the 7.5% growth rate we've been using, and enter your timeframe until retirement, i.e., 20 years. You could see some serious numbers that may compel you to consider changing your current car buying algorithm!

If you're young enough, this type of car buying and investing might even create enough wealth to pay for every car you ever purchase during your lifetime, as well as someone's college tuition! And a boat!

Not done yet… The next idea takes reducing your car payment a step further, by *eliminating it all together.* What if you considered completely forgoing that payment, opting for a less expensive model and *no debt* so that you could save more? Potentially a LOT more.

For instance, *one can opt for a $500 monthly car payment throughout their working career and have zero dollars waiting in an investment account upon retirement, or they can pay cash for more reasonable vehicles, invest that $500 monthly, and perhaps have a **fortune** building and waiting for their (much more exciting and secure) future.*

How big of a fortune are we talking about here? <u>The potential for ridiculously large bigness</u>…. Investing $500 monthly:

*(DRUMROLL, PLEASE)*

**10-year investment savings = $87,764**

**20-year investment savings = $268,647**

**30-year investment savings = $641,453**

**40-year investment savings = $1,409,817**

*CYMBAL!!!! CYMBAL AGAIN!!!!!*

*MARCHING BAND!!*

*CONFETTI!!*

*DISNEYLAND!!!*

*WHITE HOUSE!!!*

*MAGAZINE COVER!!!*

*LATE NIGHT TV APPEARANCES!!!*

*PAPARAZZI!!!*

WOW. *Some of you could join the MILLIONAIRE CLUB!!!* And your eyes are not deceiving you. By making one change, altering how you pay for your car or truck, your future can be transformed to include a wonderfully huge chest of treasure.

And while this incredible evolution was taking place, nothing really changed except the price of the vehicles you purchased and *how you paid for them.* You put an end to borrowing money.

You already had proven that you could afford to put $500 per month toward *something. You can choose to* **pay interest** *on each monthly car payment, OR you can* <u>invest</u> *your money monthly and* **be the one earning the interest.**

How would you accomplish this monumental change? You might need to build a savings balance to pay off any difference in the amount owed on your current vehicle that you would turn in to the dealer, as well as to pay cash for the new car. (Having cash on hand may not have been feasible until you picked this book up. You can soon have money in your bank!)

Again, if your payment is significantly different from the $500 number, you can do the math on our website by entering your current monthly payment amount and the 7.5% growth rate, and enter your timeframe until retirement, i.e., 20 years. You could see some serious numbers that may compel you to consider changing your current car buying system altogether!

Eliminating a car payment may not be an easy change to make. While this book attempts to find non-sacrificial modalities for the enhancement of futures, for the right person and situation, it would certainly alter the trajectory of their future.

If you haven't been able to take care of that future yet, and you're financing vehicles, give these ideas some serious thought! You are probably aware that debt is one of the great barriers to financial freedom. With that said, the choice for every single savings opportunity in this book will always be yours!

*Convert your debt into an income producer!!!*

## Autos, cont'd:  Do You Really Need 2?

Do you or does your family have a second car that isn't being driven every day? Maybe you use it just a few times a month?  What if you sold it, (don't laugh yet), and agreed to take an Uber/Lyft, cab or even rent a car when occasionally needed?

You could cut significant expenses including insurance/gas/title/repairs/parking and others in exchange for the potentially lower cost of being driven by your own hired driver. (Think of all the work, texting, sightseeing, or even napping you could accomplish while being driven around!)

Analyze your own numbers, and you just might see a significant savings…. Let's suggest the following expenses are in place for an occasionally driven (once or twice a week?) mid-size, 5-year-old vehicle worth $20,000.  The sample numbers below will vary depending on your personal situation, i.e., the state you live in, value of vehicle, etc.  Tweak them as you go along:

-Insurance; $1,000 annually

-Fuel; one fill up per month at $40 =$480 per year, let's round up to $500 to keep the math simple.

-Repairs; a check of three reliable sources estimated annual auto repairs at $400, $800, and $1,000 respectively.  We'll call it $500 annually for repairs.

-Title, Registration; Could be $200 annually but will vary by state.

-Parking; At $25 dollars a month, that's $300 per year.

Adding up these numbers, the annual expense is $2,500, or $208.33 monthly.

Next, what would you spend on hired transportation monthly? With one vehicle, you might find yourself chauffeuring more often. Even so, if someone in your family needed to hire eight rides monthly, (4 trips back and forth), at a $15 average, there's $120/month.  Thus, subtracting $120 from the $208 expense of ownership above, in this example you could save about $88 dollars monthly.

Wait, we're not done with savings yet, there is one more number and it's a big one:  You sell your second car for cash!  There's (for instance) $20k for your bank account!

You might be excited enough in a moment to tell your friends that you're about to be a one-car family!   And why would you be excited???  Well, by making this move, you're double dipping your investment opportunity.  You could put that $20k sale amount into your investment account, (growing and compounding) as well as saving (in this example) $88 monthly vs. your current second auto expense.  Let's take a look at this potentially *bursting suitcase full of money!*

$20,000 initial investment:

10-year projected savings = $41,221

20-year projected savings = $84,957

30-year projected savings = $175,099

40-year projected savings = $360,885


And, $88 invested monthly for:

10-year projected savings = $15,448

20-year projected savings = $47,285

30-year projected savings = $112,903

40-year projected savings = $248,143


Big question for you; If you sold your 2nd car, knowing that you could potentially seal the deal on a comfortable retirement savings with it, but only if you invested your profit from the sale of the second car, would you have the willpower to let that money work for you?

If that's a yes, let's add the two investments up. Both the savings from the vehicle sale and the monthly savings for not having to pay for that vehicle, <u>combined:</u>

10-year projected savings = $56,669

20-year projected savings = $132,242

30-year projected savings = $288,002

40-year projected savings = $609,028

If you happen to be in the '10 years to go until retirement' camp, this could be a **great fit** for you and a way to quickly pack your retirement account with needed dollars! Especially if you have kids who are out of the house, and you aren't driving that second car as much.

There could be disbelief on the bigger numbers, for the 20, 30, 40-year crowds. "You're suggesting that if I sell one of my cars, I could have that much money in the bank at my retirement age?" If the sample numbers are applicable to your situation, and if your investments grow as planned, then yes! Put that $20k or *your* vehicle's potential sale amount to work and agree that you won't touch it. It can be a home run, even a *grand slam* for you and your family!

What if in your situation you have calculated that you won't save any money monthly. Should you walk away from the idea? You are still suddenly saving and investing the value from the sale of your second vehicle, *and* you now have money in the bank!

Some of you may be able to enact this for a portion of your career timeframe, which can still make an impact.

Crunch your own amounts! Go to findyourhiddentreasurechest.com for both of your computations. Input the $20,000 or your estimate for selling the vehicle in the 'Initial Investment' column, 7.5% growth rate, and then insert the $88 or your estimated monthly savings in the 'Monthly Contribution' space, ensuring the frequency is monthly. Simple! And potentially life changing!!

*How about a TAXI acronym? = Truly An Xcellent Investment!!!???*

## Autos, Continued:  Gasoline for that Car

While we are in a transitional period with different types of energy that can power a vehicle, for those of you who are pumping premium gasoline into your baby because your owner's manual recommends it, let's dig deeper. Your car is, of course, a special car. It is *your* special car, and when you look at it, you get an adrenaline rush. And you love your car more than many things. But do you love it enough to blow $5,000, $10,000 on it unnecessarily? (Some of you are going to answer 'Yes, yes I do love my car enough to pay that', and that's ok....)

*Breaking news:* Auto Trader reports: If your owner's manual says **premium** fuel is <u>required,</u> then you should stick with it, but your car won't blow up if you occasionally opt for regular. Now, if your owner's manual says that **premium** fuel is <u>recommended</u>, then you can use **regular gas** every day with no worries! *Notice the lingo, required vs. recommended.*

I don't want to alarm you with these savings, but if it isn't required, there can be up to a .40c per gallon difference between regular and premium gas. What can that equate to for you? The most recent statistics show that we drive an average of 14,263 miles annually.[19]

If you're driving, let's say, 1,000 miles a month, or 12,000 miles per year and getting twenty miles to the gallon, you're buying about 600 gallons of gas per year. Saving forty cents a gallon could add $240 per year into your investment fund!

Let's say you're a BMW fan. Most of their cars 'recommend' premium gasoline. If all the cars you drove for the next 30 years were recommended, but not required to have premium gasoline, and if you changed your thinking and switched from 89 to 87 octane, 40 years from now, what could that do for you?

If you diverted that $240, ($20 monthly) savings into your investment account, you could potentially have $56,410 more dollars waiting for you in your future chest of treasure. That's almost enough to help you buy another premium luxury car (well, used, of course) with CASH! $20 savings per month:

10-year projected savings: $3,513

20-year projected savings: $10,750

30-year projected savings: $25,667

40-year projected savings: $56,410

*Fill more than your gas tank!*


### Autos, Continued: Oil Changes

This topic applies to all vehicle owners, but especially those who drive a lot. Before you pull into any Oil Change Center, do a quick internet search on your cell phone for their 'Coupons' and you should be able to save $5-10 dollars instantly, every time. I used to drive a

[19] Susan Meyer, "Average miles driven per year in the U.S.," The Zebra, August 31, 2023, https://www.thezebra.com/resources/driving/average-miles-driven-per-year/

lot and if I followed the manufacturer's recommendations, I would need 5-8 oil changes per year. Saving $5-10 per would lead to between $25-80 savings per year. We could pick an average of $50 annually saved, or about $4 per month. But hang on a moment...

If you're behind the wheel often, and if you are a stickler with the 3,000-mile oil change recommendation, that's excellent record keeping and attention to detail. Most newer vehicles have a selection that allows one to preset the number of miles driven before a reminder appears that it's time for an oil change. There is no *requirement* to spend your money every 3,000 miles unless, of course, your car's maintenance manual REQUIRES it in print.

What interval of miles does the car manufacturer, and the oil change company *recommend* you replace your oil? Typically, 3,000 miles. It will be your decision if you would like to stretch the interval out. Do you need to stick with 3,000? Per Cars.com, 'The answer is conclusive: No, you don't, according to every auto manufacturer we've talked to.....most manufacturers recommend intervals of 7,500 miles or more...'[20]

Thus, you could consider stretching out your mileage between changes. Let's say you cut your oil changes in half by driving 6,000 miles between changes, rather than 3,000. That saves the average driver a couple of oil changes per year at about $50 each, and if you also take advantage of the available coupon discounts, (another $5 to $10 each), you're saving close to $120 per year. That leads to another $10 per month for saving and investing!

Even a tweak in how you schedule your oil changes can make a difference in what you're trying to accomplish! $10 monthly =

10-year investment savings: $1,757

---

[20] Rick Popely for Cars.com, "Do You Really Need To Change Your Oil Every 3000 Miles?", USA Today, April 1, 2019, https://www.usatoday.com/story/sponsor-story/cars-dot-com/2019/04/01/do-you-really-need-change-your-oil-every-3-000-miles/3313037002/

20-year investment savings: $5,377

30-year investment savings: $12,838

40-year investment savings: $28,214

*Get your investment account running on all cylinders!*

Quick break to revisit the idea of selecting 5-10 small opportunities that could lead to a BIG number? At this early point in the exercise, someone could have chosen to save on: oil changes, ATM fees and buying beer by the case. They are already building themselves a nice little nest egg, having sacrificed what? My friends, we have barely scratched the surface, let's keep moving!

# Chapter 15:
# The Savings Opportunities
# C Through F

### Cell Phone

I have been able to capture a better monthly rate numerous times over the years by calling customer service in search of savings. Your phone company's mission is to keep you happy and your business on board. They should demonstrate a spirit of teamwork with you.

After suffering through the voice prompts and perhaps some hold time ("Sorry, I didn't understand that. Did you call me reprehensible?") you will finally be able to pursue your objective.

"Hi, and I hope it's a good day there. The reason I'm calling is that I need to reduce my bill and am seeing commercials from other companies that promise savings. I don't really *want* to make a change because I'm happy with your service. Can we review my plan and see where we can do something?"

You could find that your data usage is averaging less, or more than the plan selected. There could also be a new or more economical plan available, as new plans are offered often. You may be able to bundle internet for a discount. (Note, this same type of call can be made to your cable company as you attempt to lower that bill).

If you're able to find, save and invest just $15 monthly it has the potential to pour an estimated $42k into your box of treasure over the next 40 years!!! $42,000 for spending 10 minutes on the phone? Yes.

See what can be accomplished when you make the call. You could easily double the $15 savings. But just $15 added to your investment account per month=

10-year projected savings: $2,635

20-year projected savings: $8,064

30-year projected savings: $19,252

40-year projected savings: $42,312

*Dialing for dollars!!!*

Not done with your phone yet... Another easy reduction in your phone bill is possible and can be even more lucrative, depending on who your current carrier is. Most of the discount phone companies you see that advertise *drastically* reduced pricing compared with the 'big 3' of AT&T, T Mobile and Verizon partner with them by leasing the same larger cellular tower networks.[21]

Thus, if you're currently paying $100, $200 or more for your family's cell phone usage, you may be able to cut your bill in *half* without losing necessary coverage.

I made the switch after years of fearing the unknown. Subsequently, the only change I noticed was the accent on my voicemail prompts. My savings were close to $80 monthly.

This switch can be dramatic toward your newer and brighter future. Saving with a smaller provider and investing, for instance $50 monthly by converting from the big company name can equal:

10-year projected savings: $8,778

20-year projected savings: $26,869

30-year projected savings: $64,153

40-year projected savings: $140,998

*Bigger is not always better!!!*

---

[21] Eli Blumenthal, "Mint Mobile, Google Fi, Xfinity Mobile, Visible: Which Wireless Networks Do Smaller Providers Use?", CNET, April 2, 2023, https://www.cnet.com/tech/mobile/mint-mobile-google-fi-xfinity-mobile-visible-which-wireless-networks-do-smaller-providers-use/

## Cell Phone Replacement

Not moving on yet from your 'handheld brain', how often do you like to upgrade your phone? It seems like some companies reinvent their cell phone every year. "What, teal??? Start the car!" If you like to upgrade each time you become 'eligible,' you are probably paying up to a $40 running premium every month in your phone bill.

Being 'eligible' might mean you can have a brand-new phone 'for free' without impacting your bill. Who wouldn't do that?? However, in many cases if you were to keep your phone past when its balance is paid off, your phone bill can be reduced by that $40 payment.

Here's how that works: 'Your smartphone is built to last more than two years, but lots of people still trade up after 24 months. Doing so can lock you into another 18 to 24 months of installment payments for that new phone — **adding $20 to $40 per month, per line to your bill**.'[22]

The math on this one is tough because many of us do need new phones every few years due to things like breakage or a full memory. But if you currently get a new phone every 2 years or so, and you can stretch that to 4 years, well now we have something: $40 more per month every 2 years out of 4. That equates to $20 per month saved. Let's look at how much money you can bank by stretching out your phone replacements over your working lifetime:

10-year projected savings: $3,513

20-year projected savings: $10,750

30-year projected savings: $25,667

40-year projected savings: $56,410

It's quite incredible and even life altering to consider what a simple change such as being more patient on getting a new phone

[22] Kelsey Sheehy, "7 Ways To Lower Your Cell Phone Bill," Nerdwallet, October 13, 2022, https://www.nerdwallet.com/article/finance/lower-cell-phone-bill

could be worth to you. All you do is invest the savings. (The 'small leaks' concept!)

*Be patient and dial up savings!*

Quick note on every single opportunity you're reviewing: It's safe to say that the savings you find **now** will change, or even disappear over the years. Does that mean you should eliminate your deposit of that amount? *Absolutely not!*

You have established a new habit of devoting savings to your investment fund. As long as you can afford it, keep pounding that initial amount toward your future, and always keep your eyes open, looking for more. Job promotions and pay raises will have you finding *more* to deposit! End sidebar!

## Childcare

Research of multiple sources makes it reasonable to estimate that the cost of raising a child to adulthood averages about $300,000 today. A big part of that expense can be childcare/daycare.

When both parents are working, childcare costs alone can surpass $1,500 monthly per munchkin unit! If you are dropping off your kid(s) at a childcare facility, consider some alternatives that could assist in repainting your financial picture! This is a personal and sensitive subject, but if you're struggling financially and dropping your kid(s) off at a daycare facility before work, give a look...

For instance, using co-ops can cut childcare costs by 75-80%! If you're able to cut a $1,000 monthly expense by $750, down to just $250, you are talking about a major windfall to your financial situation. There are also babysitting exchanges that can cut your monthly spending in half compared with typical childcare facilities. That's potentially $500 to be saved per child per month.

Do you have a reliable friend or relative taking care of their child at home who would be interested in additional income?

Investigate your options. Perhaps comfort could be found with an alternative to the current arrangement which reduces your childcare costs. Saving, for instance, $300 per month could lead to:

10-year projected savings: $52,659

Crunch your own numbers if you find something suitable!

We've assumed just one child for this example and let's hope that you're not paying childcare costs for decades. But wait! You're not done building your stockpile of valuables yet. How so? Using the example above, in 10 years you could amass a projected $52,659 that you've saved in your investment account! Let's suppose you were 25 when you had your first child, and for the next 10 years, you saved and invested that $300 monthly savings on your childcare expenses that you would have paid had you not made the change.

So, fast forward 10 years later, and you no longer need the help of childcare services. And you now have the above $52,659 in your portfolio from investing your monthly childcare savings! You're now 35 years old, and you're planning to work for about another 30 years.

Let's see what happens when you *LEAVE THAT $52,659 IN YOUR INVESTMENT ACCOUNT, GROWING AND COMPOUNDING FOR 30 MORE YEARS UNTIL YOU RETIRE:*

What could happen? **$461,027**, that's what could happen! *This is the projected value of your $52,659 investment that grows at 7.5% per year for 30 years!!! WOAH!!!!*

Note that this concept applies to any investment that you deposit and allow to grow and compound! It could multiply many times depending on your growth rate and the length of time you have it invested!

Now, back to that monthly expense: Once you were beyond the need for childcare, what if you *then* diverted that $300 expense into your investment account? You no longer need to spend it on childcare, correct?

Let's see where *that* road leads and we can add that projected number to the future value of the estimated $52,659 you've already saved. If you now begin investing the $300 monthly, here's where your total balance, including the saved $52k could be in another 30 years; $461,027 plus $384,875 ($300 monthly for 30 years):

30-year projected savings: $845,902

Good grief, one could nearly be a *millionaire* in another 30 years from this opp alone! Crunch your own numbers!

*Who knew your kids could be so valuable!!!*

## Cigarettes

The stop-smoking category goes against our concept of avoiding sacrifice or change. But it is very much worth including. How do I know? I used to smoke.

If you are a smoker, I know you have looked for reasons to quit. Let's add another: The median price for a pack of cigarettes is $7.93.[23] Let's average this at $7.50 for our example, which means a pack-a-day habit could set the smoker back $225 per month or $2,700 per year.

If you smoke and don't have any savings yet, what if you took that $2,700 annual spend, and looked at those smokes and had a talk with them? "It's either you or my family's big comfortable treasure chest and retirement."

Want to see what a difference this can make? What you're about to see is highly compelling financial support for quitting this habit!!!

In 30 years, not only will you have a better chance to be alive and in good health, you can then also be looking at **just under $300,000**

---

[23] 'Cigarette Prices by State 2023,' *World Population Review*, Nov. 27, 2023, https://worldpopulationreview.com/state-rankings/cigarette-prices-by-state

**dollars** in added security for your family.  The additional side benefits of better health and a longer life are icing on the cake, allowing you more time to enjoy that duffel bag full of money!

Now, what if you're married and you both smoke?  If you both quit now, and let's say you're in your mid 30's, and you invest those savings, you could have *CLOSE TO $600,000 DOLLARS IN THE BANK WHEN YOU'RE 65.*

What if you're 25, and quit right now?  You take that estimated $228 you're spending every month and begin an automatic transfer of that amount from your paycheck into your retirement fund.  You'll have an estimated **$642,886 dollars waiting for you in 40 years when you're 65!!!!  And if you're also married to a smoker and both stop, <u>double that number to almost $1.3 million.</u>  Quit while you're young and let that great decision fund your secure and wonderful future as a reward.**

If you've been looking for that last push to get you over the edge, that *one more thing* aside from your health, aside from future medical issues and a shorter lifespan, the smell, the smoking out in the rain, the cough, the being out of breath, the looks you get…. **Maybe life changing dollars will do it for you!  Think of it as 'getting paid to quit.'**

You'll need to average your own monthly spend here, but if you're close to the $7.50 per pack, and pack a day expense:  $228 saved and invested per month:

10-year projected savings = $40,022

20-year projected savings = $122,505

30-year projected savings = $292,507

40-year projected savings = $642,886

(That's just for one of you).

*Instead of a cigarette, light up the path to a longer future brimming with fulfilled dreams!*

## Coffee K Cups

If you're using disposable K Cups to brew your coffee, you might have an opportunity to turn your morning cup into more than just a wake-up call. You could make a very simple switch to a reusable filter, filled with your favorite coffee, and at a strength you prefer. You could then also be adding to your wealth monthly! How much?

Well, a pound of coffee holds 64 tablespoons, and regardless of whether you would put one or two tbsps. in your reusable filter, you'll be saving money. As a side benefit, you'll also be reducing environmental waste.

The disposable K Cups might cost between .60 and a dollar each. You can brew your own for as little as .10 to .30 depending on what you buy and how much coffee you pack into the filter.

If you're drinking K Cup type coffee as well as struggling to save for your future, this could be an easy reversal for you. It would be simple enough to save $10 to $30 per month, subject to the variables above. If we split the difference and estimate $20 saved per month, there is magic to add to your retirement fund at 7.5% growth!

10-year projected savings: $3,513

20-year projected savings: $10,750

30-year projected savings: $25,667

40-year projected savings: $56,410

*Wake up and smell the money!!!*

Try to maintain a climate of cost consciousness with all you consume. Be on the lookout for opportunities that can be synergized into improving your future!

For instance, if you regularly purchase pineapple in a can or plastic container, that's an opportunity for more than just savings. Buy a whole pineapple and cut it yourself. It's easy and it's as fresh as you can get without picking your own. As a bonus you'll save a couple dollars each time!

## College Loans

If you currently have college debt, keep reading. Otherwise, feel free to skip this section.

Did you know that your college loans are typically set up like a credit card payment, requiring only the minimum payment? This stretches your loan term up to as many as 17 years until payoff, or what can feel like an eternity until the day your education really starts to get you ahead in life!

Do you know what your college loan rate is? It is far from a bargain unless you are very lucky. Many are currently at about 8% or more while home mortgage rates are currently less than that. Unless you somehow got a sweetheart of a deal, college loans are *not a great value*.

When combining the rising price of tuition, room and board, and books, the college loan can be a heavy and discouraging anchor.

For private student loans, repayment usually begins after graduation. Ironically, this buzz killing obligation arrives shortly after one of the happiest and proudest moments of your young life. A payment booklet arrives as a late graduation gift from a new surprise boss, your college loan administrator!

You may recall our coverage of compounding interest earlier, (earning money off principal *and* interest earned). When you have a college loan, *the banks are reversing and magnifying that concept on you.* How so? Well, they don't require you to start making payments on your loans until you graduate or are out of school, but you had better believe they begin charging interest as soon as your first loan is approved and paid to the school for the first semester of your freshman year.

And thus, for that first loan you received in your freshman year, by the time you graduate, your loan has interest charges added over all four years. For example, a $20,000 loan at 8% for your freshman year may have an actual balance of close to $27,000 by graduation day. And that's just the first year's loan!

Every year that a student is in school, interest is compounding each semester and year on the loans that was previously executed. While a student may be off at a toga party, their loan company is having their own celebration, making it rain as they count the multiplying returns on the interest being earned from day one of the loan.

There can be a good opportunity for you to improve your circumstances. There are companies that are in the business of refinancing college loans at a lower rate than you're currently paying your student loan provider.

Give the student loan refi companies a try. Depending on your loan balances and interest rates, you may find that you can save $50, $100, even $200 or more per month, depending on your balances. By capturing a $100 monthly savings and re-routing that money right back into paying off that loan sooner, you could seriously reduce your length of term (and interest paid) from the typical payment terms that private loan companies utilize.

Let's use an example of $100 savings, directed toward early payoff of a $20,000 student loan, which trims 2 years off a 10-year payoff. Now, let's direct that $100 for the extra 2 years into your investment account.

In 2 years your extra $100 payments from savings on the original loan now become $2,587 at an 8% growth rate. Now, what if you let that $2,587 continue working for you, invested? What would that amount become over time as you simply let it grind on its own? A one-time investment of $2,587 can become:

10-year projected savings = $5,332

20-year projected savings = $10.989

30-year projected savings = $22,649

40-year projected savings = $46,680

*Take a class in refinancing!!!*

An ironic way of looking at this opportunity is that it's possible to recapture part or all of what you spent on your education, simply by refinancing, then paying off your loans early, and ultimately letting the money you saved work for you as an investment.

Here's some added good news for your financial future. One day years from now, you'll make the final payment on your student loan(s). You would then have an extra (for instance) $200 monthly 'pay raise' available to divert to your investment portfolio. That amount can make you quite wealthy depending on your age. Remember to do the right thing with those dollars!

If you have student loans and have never taken the time to shop them around, investigate this one, as it could positively affect your financial life. Search 'student loan refinance' and you'll be on your way.

While we're on the subject, what if you're a single Mom or Dad and are hoping to cover some or all your child's future higher education expenses? You could enroll in a 529 plan to save for that purpose, and some of them have good interest rates. By investing $100 monthly for the next 20 years on your own, you could have more than $50,000 available to turn that noble thought into reality. Your total contribution could be less than half of that total!


## Credit Cards: Points, Miles, Cash Back, Balance Transfers, Offers

First rule with credit cards; NEVER pay interest!!! Charge only what you know you can pay off at the end of the month!!!

Next, if you charge items every month and are not earning cash back, miles, or hotel points with your credit card(s) now, *you can add a simple opportunity to collect these benefits.* My pal Steve has shown me the way on this idea. Most companies offer these options to entice you with additional perks to keep their card competitive, and you MUST take advantage of this…. Free flights and cash back for using your credit cards can add some spice, as well as cash savings, to your life!

Switching to another topic on charge cards, many of us have had them for years. If you have debt on a credit card that charges interest, and if your credit is decent enough, (about 670 or higher[24]), 'Transferring a high-interest balance to a credit card with a 0% introductory rate can save you hundreds or even thousands of dollars in interest, money you can apply toward getting out of debt sooner.'[25]

Look into the available options if you have credit balance(s)! If you're able to transfer a balance and save on interest charges, the savings amount should first be used to accelerate your payments to pay off the debt on that card, and *then* be directed straight into your investment account!

Another nice benefit of many credit cards; By logging into your account and clicking on 'benefits' or 'offers', you can also take advantage of free offers from numerous companies, promoting discounts at places such as Starbucks, Walmart grocery, discounts on flowers, restaurants, and dozens of other companies that offer additional discounts simply because you purchase those products and pay with your card. Just click 'get offer.'

---

[24] Bev O'Shea, "Pros and Cons of Balance Transfer Cards, Experian, September 21, 2023, https://www.experian.com/blogs/ask-experian/pros-cons-balance-transfer-credit-cards/#:~:text=You%20May%20Need%20a%20High,now%20on%20your%20other%20debt.

[25] Nerd Wallet, "Start Saving Money ASAP: Pay No Intro Interest For Up To 18 Months," November 9, 2023, https://www.nerdwallet.com/m/credit-cards/pay-0-intro-interest?bucket_id=LP2&gad=1&gclid=CjwKCAjwzo2mBhAUEiwAf7wjkgRwm13Vq6llCsVCoz6xe0J9gjcbPLJ_CFUhEBAj9tm926cHdSkVRoCgU0QAvD_BwE&gclsrc=aw.ds&mktg_body=1678&mktg_hline=11649&mktg_img=3599&mktg_place=aud-366608404463%3Akwd-5343485737&model_execution_id=4D3AAB0E-828E-4B40-966B-1FE01FB018DB&nw_campaign_id=150238292830084300&utm_campaign=cc_mktg_paid_071520_balancetransfer_beta&utm_content=ta&utm_medium=cpc&utm_source=goog&utm_term=what+is+a+credit+card+balance+transfer

Can doing this save you $5 per month??? Very reasonable and you'll probably save a lot more than that. (I have gotten $50 back just for booking a certain hotel I needed to stay at anyway). If you order flowers online during the year, this can save you $$, even on top of the other floral discounts you might use.

A microscopic $5 per month invested will add almost $7,500 into your retirement account over the next 30 years. Again, all it took was to click 'get offer'. Check your card's online account regularly for new offers. You can benefit from items that you would have purchased anyway, so why not?

Most of us will be using a credit card for the rest of our lives, yes? For those on the 40-year plan, clicking on these offers and saving just $5 monthly could lead to a whopping investment savings estimated to be over $17k!!!

All you must do is add the $5 into the monthly automatic transfer we'll be creating for your investment account, or simply increase your contribution if you already have one working in your favor! Just $5 monthly:

10-year projected savings: $880

20-year projected savings: $2,691

30-year projected savings: $6,423

40-year projected savings: $14,116

*The credit all goes to you! This is small but remember, 'small leaks'... a group of little ones become significant!*


### Dog, Pet Grooming

Do you pay someone to pamper your dog? This service might cost about $75 for each groomer visit, and typically gets scheduled to recur every 6 weeks. Let's do some math! That's about 8-1/2 doggie stylings per year. That's $637.50 spent annually, and counting tips and Christmas, could approach $750 spent annually to have Spot looking spot-on!

Now, I have loved each and every one of my dogs, but if you had told me that I could be giving up nearly $90,000 in investment savings to pay for their grooming over the years, I might have bought hamsters instead... If you're young and own a dog, look at the 40-year number and imagine the possibilities if you were to take care of their grooming *and were sure to invest what you saved.*

There is no denying that the dog groomer does a fantastic job. The dog looks better, smells pretty for at least a day or two, and some other services are provided, such as nail clipping and backside expression things.

Remember, if you don't like an idea, just move on! It's that easy and is always up to you to decide if an idea is worthy. By grooming your own pet, check out the possibilities:

$750 divided by 12 months = $62.50 saved per month. $63 invested monthly:

10-year projected savings = $11,060

20-year projected savings = $33,853

30-year projected savings = $80,831

40-year projected savings = $177,653

*Sit! Lay down! Roll over! Prosper!!! Travel!!!*


## Drive-Thru Instant Coffee Syndrome

If you're in this group and struggling to make ends meet, this is a real opportunity that can be implemented without too much pain: Instant Coffee Syndrome, (not the kind that you pour boiling water into, the other trendy coffee that you drive your car through, accessorized with foo-foo, and potentially iced).

If you enjoy purchasing a barista-crafted $5 cup of coffee on your way to work every morning, with or without getting out of your car, take a moment to do the math on what you're spending. 22 workdays = $110 per month which is around $1,330 spent per year on coffee. Not counting weekends.

You know the drill... Are you ready for these calculations??? Over 40 years, by investing that money monthly instead, you could realize considerable wealth of over **$280,000.** If your target is 30 years, you could be near **$130,000.** Even over just 10 years, you may be able to amass close to $18,000!

Try this instead and make it fun: Go to your grocery store and look in the coffee section. There's usually a two-for-one or discounted coffee deal there. Get two $8-$10 bags of quality premium coffee for the price of one, which should last you at least a month. You could make a game out of buying the different coffees that are on sale and have your own 'coffee of the month' experience! Every coffee manufacturer offers numerous varieties, and they all seem to take turns going on sale. You can even ice them!

So, let's suggest about $100 saved per month, ($110 saved minus $10 spent). You just saved over a thousand dollars annually by reducing the $1,330 you spend annually down to an estimated $120 dollars per year. Now splurge! Buy yourself a cool coffee maker and a nice expensive coffee mug. You earned it!!! Let's see what $100 per month looks like when invested.

10-year projected savings: $17,555

20-year projected savings: $53,733

30-year projected savings: $128,298

40-year projected savings: $281,978

*Savings that could eliminate the jitters!!!*

## Electricity/Lights

If you really want to get down to microeconomics, let's talk light bulbs! Humor this topic for just a moment. The average cost of having an *incandescent* light bulb on is about 0.6 cents per hour.[26] That's peanuts, right???

Do you find yourself keeping lights on in the house even when you're not using them? Do you have some switches that turn on 4-5-6 lights or more, such as in the kitchen or living room?

Tip: If you can find and turn off 5 lights for an extra 10 hours a day, savings of about 3 cents a day per light can be realized, times 10 hours = 30 cents a day. 30 cents times 30 days =$9 saved per month. Or $108 per year. So, take that $9 monthly savings and make sure to include that number in your monthly transfer for your investment allocation, and the magic you see below happens. It may be hard to imagine this being possible, but the numbers don't lie! Let's round up to $10 per month, (you can add another dollar into your savings):

10-year investment savings: $1,757

20-year investment savings: $5,377

30-year investment savings: $12,838

40-year investment savings: $28,214

*Bright idea!*


## Electricity/Upgrade Your Light Bulbs

If you still use incandescent lights and are interested in upgrading those bulbs to LEDs, you can realize an upgrade in your retirement

---

[26] "How Much Does It Cost To Leave A Light On For 24 Hours?" Electric Rate, January 27, 2023, https://www.electricrate.com/how-much-does-it-cost-to-leave-a-light-on-for-24-hours/

account as well. LEDs are also better for the environment, as they're more energy efficient and aren't toxic.

'If you currently have 30 bulbs at home, you can save up to $200 in a year if you upgrade all bulbs to LEDs.'[27] And what does $200 invested annually look like? We'll round down to $15 saved monthly:

10-year projected savings: $2,635

20-year projected savings: $8,064

30-year projected savings: $19,252

40-year projected savings: $42,312

There could be a sizable initial investment for LEDs, but after that it's all annual savings.

*An even brighter idea!!!*

## Exterminator

If you're paying for this service, consider becoming the one who keeps your home and yard insect free. Doing this could take a little studying. Note that we're not including termite prevention and inspection here, nor removal of varmints, only typical insect pest control.

As a side benefit, if you choose to treat pests yourself, you can know exactly what types of substances your family, friends and pets will be exposed to in your home.

---

[27] "How Much Does It Cost To Leave A Light On," ElectricRate, January 7, 2023, https://www.electricrate.com/how-much-does-it-cost-to-leave-a-light-on-for-24-hours/

If you currently pay for a monthly service, research shows you might be spending $30-50 per treatment on average.[28] If you're getting treatments every two months, it's closer to $50- $60, six times per year, or about $300-$360 annually.

If taking this work on by yourself, the cost of pesticides you might use could be close to $50 annually in a normal size home. One checked source found the cost per year to be as low as just $1.58 annually![29] But let's use the $50 number, and we'll suppose you can save at least $20 per month, or $240 per year.

While being your own pest control 'technician' might not seem like the professional treatment you're getting, with some homework you may be able to do a safe, admirable job, as well as have the ability to be immediately responsive if-and-when a need for a spot treatment arises. $20 saved monthly =

10-year projected savings: $3,513

20-year projected savings: $10,750

30-year projected savings: $25,667

40-year projected savings: $56,410

*Invest while you divest your pest guests!!!*

## Fitness Club, Gym Memberships

Hopefully, fitness and good health are among your plans as you build your fortune. Once you have accumulated a bank account stuffed with money, you'll want to be in great health to live longer and enjoy what you've saved, right??? Well, if fitness clubs are

---

[28] Shane Sentelle, "How Much Does Pest Control Cost (2023)," Architectural Digest, November 7, 2023, https://www.architecturaldigest.com/reviews/pest-control/pest-control-cost

[29] Joel, "Should You Do Your Own Pest Control?" How To Money, October 20, 2023, https://www.howtomoney.com/do-it-yourself-pest-control-will-save-you-big-money/

already a part of your routine, there are methods to help save money on memberships, just as with nearly *everything* you consume.

As a member of a health club, even though you may have already signed a contract, you may be able to save.

-Add a friend or family for a discount.

-Request a trial membership of a different membership level.

-Offer to pay in advance or to commit to a longer term for a discount on the monthly rate.

-Check and see if discounts are available if you come in during off-peak hours. Some clubs offer this if you're OK with working out at less popular hours.

-Check with your employer or healthcare company to see if they have any group membership deals. (You might even have a membership open to you at no charge via your company's medical plan).

-Research today's specials. Newer, better programs can give you bargaining power.

Try to re-negotiate your current contract. "I like this club, but there are some great deals on others, what can you do? Can we revisit my contract and see if there are any options that can save money?" Managers should want to find a way to keep you onboard.

If you take the time to research and negotiate, you could save $20 per month, if not more...

$20 monthly savings:

10-year projected savings: $3,513

20-year projected savings: $10,750

30-year projected savings: $25,667

40-year projected savings: $56,410

*You'll need to stay strong to be able to haul your treasure chest around!!!*


### Fitness Club, Gym Memberships, cont'd

There is another group holding these memberships who have an excellent savings opportunity. USA Today reports that a full 67 percent of gym memberships go completely unused. But even among those who do use their gym membership, many are not exactly what you'd call regulars.[30]

If you fit into the above group definition, there might be a better option that you *will* use, such as creating a small space at your home where you can add equipment and do your good work without leaving the house.

Eliminating wasteful spending wherever you're able just makes good sense. While difficult to quantify individual costs and plans, to suggest a savings opportunity of $40 monthly for terminating your fitness contract is not unreasonable and can make a big addition to your wealth desires.

10-year projected savings: $7,023

20-year projected savings: $21,496

30-year projected savings: $51,324

40-year projected savings: $112,802

*Work it out!!!*

---

[30] "What Percentage of Gym Memberships Go Unused?", Exercise.com, November 10, 2023, https://www.exercise.com/grow/unused-gym-memberships-percentage/

## Flowers

Do you buy flowers throughout the year for Valentine's Day, Mother's Day, and other events? Do you go online and order? First, if you're taking advantage of the credit card offers in the earlier credit card section, you'll save money, usually 10-20%, or between $5 and $20 per occurrence if you spend between $50 and $100 on an order of flowers.

Next, do an internet search for discounts, and you could double dip the savings! By saving another $5 - $20 per order, and let's say flowers are ordered at least three times per year, (Valentine's Day, Mother's Day, and another), one could save up to $60 annually.

Even though it's a tiny amount, don't forget it! In fact, these little opportunities are easy to overlook. A handful of small amounts can add up to make a significant difference in your investment account! (Take them very seriously!) Just $5 monthly can equal:

10-year projected savings: $880

20-year projected savings: $2,691

30-year projected savings: $6,423

40-year projected savings: $14,116

*Ah, the fragrant smell of cash!!!*

**Fact Check:** If I direct just $5 monthly into an investment account, could it really add up to more than $10,000 over the next 40 years??? True or false?

At a 7.5% annual growth rate, in 40 years you're projected to have $14,116 in your portfolio.

**Fact Check Results:** True! Think long term and think big!

The example above could become a 2-week excursion to Spain, Hawaii, Italy or wherever you wish to travel. Or a used car or boat. Or furniture or a kitchen upgrade. For investing $5 per month…

Most of these ideas require little effort to incorporate. Add 3-4-5-10 more of these insignificant numbers to your monthly savings amount and see what happens!

## Greeting Cards

There might be a nice card included with the flowers. I learned this one from observing my mom over the years. Are you currently buying your $5 to $10 cards individually at the grocery or drug store? If so, try going to your dollar store and buy 25-50 assorted greeting cards. That's right, they're about $1 each. And they are good quality. This is EASILY hundreds of dollars saved annually if you like sending cards to your family and friends. By purchasing in advance, you're ready for any occasion even on short notice, ("Holy cow, tomorrow is Fruitcake Toss Day?!"), and you're saving money! You might want better cards for significant remembrances, such as Valentine's Day, your spouse's birthday, or Mother's Day, (we've made a case for times when discounts may not be the best option....). But do the math: How many greeting cards do you buy annually now? Have you ever counted? It could be a *long* list.

If you're saving $5 or more per card, and buying just one card per month, this option could become something meaningful in your pocket tomorrow! It's another 'little' 5 bucks per month to invest! Practice this tactic and over the next 40 years, *boom!*

10-year projected savings = $880

20-year projected savings = $2,691

30-year projected savings = $6,423

40-year projected savings = $14,116

*Send yourself a 'Congrats!' card for your good fortune!*

# Chapter 16:
## The Savings Opportunities
## G Through K

### Groceries

Everyone buys groceries, so we'll spend a little extra time here with multiple ways to produce savings.

1) Purchase the lower cost options. Look for the generic or store brands right next to many of the big brand names. These items may have been produced and generically packaged by that name brand! If you haven't already, give them a try. Sometimes you might find that the generic brand doesn't measure up, but then again, sometimes it's just fine or even better!

2) Buy One Get One Free. If your grocery store has '2 for the price of 1' sales, if you can afford it, spend the extra money and stock up every time you see products you know you'll use. If you see 'BOGO' items available that you don't use regularly, it's probably best not to take advantage, as you'll may end up throwing out expired food/items down the road. I'm not saying I would ever do that, but I've heard it can happen:).

As an example, challenge yourself to save at least $20 at the grocery store for every $100 spent, by purchasing common items you'll use that are sale items or '2 for 1'. You don't have to look very hard; they're well marked. Your receipt should show your savings. Challenge yourself to make the amount saved a big number each time.

Let's say you've made your grocery list and are interested in finding a nice steak for tonight's dinner. As you're looking at the beef section you notice a discount tag on the chicken next door. You see that you can feed the family for half the cost if you change your menu. Boom, done, and saved.

As you shop, always keep at least one eye scanning for items you know you'll consume. Even if you don't need it this week, you might save $7 on a pack of frozen shrimp that's on sale which can go into the freezer until you are ready to use it. That will keep you from paying full price when you issue your dinner edict; "I demand shrimp diablo tonight!"

Let's talk about perishables, as there might be a small recapture opportunity available to you in that department. Things like fruit, veggies, cereal, dairy; Monitor what you throw out for a while, and you'll see a pattern. For instance, we NEVER have to throw expired milk out, but the fruit drawer will often become a science experiment. We don't notice it until it begins to glow. And occasionally, a box of our cereal goes stale. That can be a fun surprise on your first spoonful...!

Let's suggest that if you make the extra effort, you can hone your savings by $5 per week, or $20 per month. (There is much more to be saved than that, but we'll start there. I'll also list the $40 per month investment savings, because some of you can save that much and more):

$20 monthly savings:

10-year projected savings: $3,513

20-year projected savings: $10,750

30-year projected savings: $25,667

40-year projected savings: $56,410


$40 monthly savings:

10-year projected savings: $7,023

20-year projected savings: $21,496

30-year projected savings: $51,324

40-year projected savings: $112,802

*Don't put your money where your mouth is!!!*

## Grocery and Meal Delivery

If you are already struggling to make ends meet, it is doubtful that you are utilizing these services, as they cost more than doing the shopping and prep yourself, and you can be contracted into painful monthly payments. With that said, this service is a popular option today. This is typically a subscription service.

For those of you who can afford this convenience, some require the purchase of about ten meals per week minimum, averaging about $10 per meal. That's around $100 per week, or $400 per month spent.

The question is, how much does it cost when you shop and cook for yourself, by comparison, or how expensive were your meals before you contracted this service? Only you know that answer, but there are a couple of facts that should lead to savings if you do it yourself: With meal delivery, it may be more convenient and the food might be delicious, but you're paying extra for food preparation, packaging of individual meals, and shipping, not to mention advertising, inventory and other costs incurred and passed on by your meal service company.

Even if the difference is only $2 per meal, let's do the math: Assuming your meal plan is like what's described above and requires about ten meals delivered per week, that's $20 that could be saved each week, or $80 per month.

It is understood that you wouldn't be considering using a meal service for the next 20-30-40 years. Remember though, once you begin investing your saved money, you will continue forever unless you can't, right? $80 per month:

10-year projected savings: $14,044

20-year projected savings: $42,987

30-year projected savings: $102,640

40-year projected savings: $225,586

*Buy your own groceries and reduce your growth worries. (If you try hard enough it kind of rhymes).*

## Grocery Apps

If you don't mind shopping at multiple stores in your area, there are new grocery apps such as Flashfood that can help you find and save as much as 50% on groceries! Let's not put a number on this opp, but if *you* use it and save, add that money into you-know-where!

*Save even more at the grocery store!!!*

## Groceries, Online Coupons

The average grocery shopper could save more than $300 per year by using online coupons for at home purchases.[31] If you utilize this benefit, and if your savings fall near the average, you could save and then invest $25 per month! That is not small money:

10-year projected savings: $4,390

20-year projected savings: $13,436

30-year projected savings: $32,081

40-year projected savings: $70,508

*Gold mine online!!!*

---

[31] Beth Braverman, David Schiff, Amanda Gengler, "90 Great Ways to Save," AARP Bulletin July/August 2023, Vol. 64, No. 6, https://advertise.aarp.org/uploads/misc/JulAug-23.pdf

## Heat and A/C

What temperature do you keep your thermostat at in the summer? How about winter? What if you adjusted it just a little? Why? "The Department of Energy estimates **savings** of about 1 percent for each degree of **thermostat** adjustment per 8 hours and recommends **turning thermostats** back 7 to 10 degrees from their normal settings for 8 hours per day to achieve annual **savings** of **up** to 10%."[32]

It may not seem reasonable to turn your thermostat down 7 to 10 degrees at night. So, let's say you turn it down one degree during the day, and just 4 degrees at night. Or some similar combination. You have blankets and covers if it's a little chillier than normal. And you may enjoy the feeling of getting under the covers and warming up. Anyway, I digress… But that's about a 5-degree difference, or about a 5% lowering of your energy bill. What does that mean? Well, how much is your energy bill? 'The **typical** American **family** spends at least $2,200 on energy **bills** every year.'[33]

OK, now we have a basis to work from. Taking 5% off that $2,200 spent annually equates to $110 dollars per year. Not bad, but doesn't sound earth-shattering, right??

Now, let's get thinking longer term like we've been discussing, because you're not just going to do this for a month. How much longer do you expect to work? Let's say the answer is 40 years.

If you do the math, and you make the mentioned adjustment above and stick with it, (it might take a few days to adjust and then you could

---

[32] Josh Crank, "How Much Can You Save By Adjusting Your Thermostat?", Direct Energy Blog, Apr 10, 2018

 https://blog.directenergy.com/how-much-can-you-save-by-adjusting-your-thermostat/

[33] Dan Ketchum, "How Much Will It Cost Me To Run An Air Conditioner?" budgeting.thenest.com, November 1, 2018, https://budgeting.thenest.com/much-cost-run-air-conditioner-23306.html

forget it even happened.). On your way to bed, you'll just turn down the thermostat by habit, or if you have a programmable model, make the one-time adjustment.

Now let's look at what happens to your money when you invest that $9 a month earning a reasonable average of 8% per year. Let's round up by a dollar (you can afford a dollar, yes?) and call it $10 per month. That's right, you'll see that saving $120 a year, or $10 per month by adjusting your thermostat will cause a rise in temperature in your future! You could have an estimated $28,214 waiting for you in 40 years.

10-year investment savings: $1,757

20-year investment savings: $5,377

30-year investment savings: $12,838

40-year investment savings: $28,214

*That should warm your heart.*

This is an illustration of how another small change can help to contribute to a BIG retirement income. Nearly all of us have heating and cooling bills. This is a ridiculously frugal change, but it can become a monster for you!! Look at the 40-year number. If you happen to be 25 years old now, you can have a large stack of Franklins waiting for you when that 40-year period has passed.

And, speaking of Ben Franklin, he mused, 'Beware of the little expenses, a small leak will sink a great ship.'[34] That can be reworded to say, 'The little expenses can add up to a great ship.' Try finding ten ways to save just $10 per month. Then invest that $100. It could indeed become a great ship for you to sail off in!

For those of you who only want to work another 10 years, let's look at lowering your thermostat even more, and perhaps working

---

[34] "Thoughts on the Business of Life," Forbes Quotes, December 8, 2023, https://www.forbes.com/quotes/1098/

even harder at your number. You too can have a nice stash waiting for you in just 10 years by making this and other small adjustments.

## Heating a Room, cont'd

We're not done with heating and cooling just yet. Here's another place to save on your Heat and Air Conditioning bill. Do you keep doors open to rooms that rarely get used? Guest bedrooms? Basement? A bathroom?

Cost savings can be a little tricky when trying to nail down an exact figure, because they will vary by type and size of house, type of furnace, insulation, climate, and type of furnace and fuel you're using (in order of least expensive energy to most expensive; heat pump, natural gas, oil, propane, electric baseboard)[35]. But…. There is money to be saved!

So, let's attempt to find a general average for closing a door and the vent to a standard 10 x 12 room in a 2,200 square foot home.

On average it costs $2,146 per year to heat a 2,200 square foot home. If you eliminate heating 120 square feet, that's about 5.5% of the area and total energy cost.

We can thus calculate a savings of about $121 per year, or about $10 monthly per room of that size.

What about the warm months when you want A/C? Depending on where you live, and if you have heat and air conditioning in your house, you're probably using a combination of the two throughout the year.

---

[35] Copyrighting Team, "The Real Cost of Heating," Energy Services Group, June 24, 2019, https://www.energysvc.com/the-real-cost-of-heating/

'It costs an *average* of $165 per month to cool the average size home with a 3-ton A/C unit.'[36] Let's again take 5.5% of the cost for the 10 X 12 room: That brings us a similar monthly savings number: $9.08. The cost of both heat and air are similar in this example!

Thus, if you have an average size house of 2,200 square feet, you might be able to knock about $10 off your monthly bill *just by closing off one seldom used room.*

Here's what closing off a room could do for your banking and investment account. Got an open guest bedroom? Close that door and save and invest $10 monthly:

10-year investment savings: $1,757

20-year investment savings: $5,377

30-year investment savings: $12,838

40-year investment savings: $28,214

*It's getting hot in here…!!!*

Add this example to the thermostat adjustment savings, and you are creating more significant investment numbers. That's right, by tightening your heat and A/C usage, you can have a more sizable savings growing and waiting for you when you need it. What if you find out you can close off two rooms or more? Wow.

Another *tiny* change that could equal a greater than tiny result. Let's keep going!

---

[36] "How Much Will It Cost Me To Run My Air Conditioner?" Sears Heating and Cooling, November 10, 2023, Https://www.searsheatingcooling.com/cost-to-run-air-conditioner/

## Home Improvements

I've always told my wife "I'm not afraid to try and fix anything around the house, as long as you're ok with imperfection." Over the last 5 years, I have remodeled the plumbing of two bathrooms, installed landscape lights, a large awning, enclosed a room, completed some crazy car repairs I didn't know I was capable of, installed ceiling fans, and other projects. All these jobs could have been farmed out.

The internet is a wonderful teaching tool! You can often watch someone else do exactly what you need to do, and then do it yourself!

The difference between the estimates to have those jobs done for me, minus my expense and doing them myself is thousands of dollars.

If you can save just a few hundred dollars a year by taking care of what's breaking in your home, rather than contracting it out, you can put that saved money right into your fund where it can multiply! Keep in mind that most services could cost you close to $100 an hour just in labor. If you can do your own plumbing job that saves a 3-hour labor charge, you are making a great $300 investment! (Rule of thumb: Regardless of the job, if it's dangerous, or if an error could be costly, pay someone else to do it. Make sure you know important facts before beginning, such as where your water main shutoff is, do you need a second person to help, do you have a backup plan and so on before you begin. Keep Murphy's Law in mind!)

Let's just pretend that about every year you take on one job around the house that you would normally contract out, and that you save 3 hours of labor or about $300. That's $25 per month. Go ahead and invest that $25 starting now. The results are in!

10-year projected savings: $4,390

20-year projected savings: $14,436

30-year projected savings: $32,081

40-year projected savings: $70,508

*A jack-of-all-trades can have it made in the shade!!!*

## Home Improvement, continued:  Pressure Washing, Carpet Cleaning, Tree Trimming, And Other Occasional Jobs

More DIY items…. You can pay hundreds to have these tasks done for you, or you can go to your local home improvement/hardware store and rent (or buy) the equipment yourself. You'll save more than half the cost of the farmed-out price.

If you want to save even more money on these occasional tasks, before you rent the equipment, knock on a few of your neighbor's doors and see if they are interested in doing the job you're looking to do. If you can get 1 or 2 other households to join in with you on a rental, not only will you save more money, but you can also help each other and knock out the jobs together.

Let's estimate one job per year that you might currently contract out, (either carpet/upholstery cleaning, pressure washing your home/driveway, window washing, etc.), at a savings of $100. Dig deep and round this up to $10 invested monthly:

10-year investment savings: $1,757

20-year investment savings: $5,377

30-year investment savings: $12,838

40-year investment savings: $28,214

*Your labor is worth more than you thought!!!*


## Home Phone

Do you still have a home phone? Why?? To be able to fax?? Because you have a contract with your security monitoring company?? For the former, you can do everything you need with a laptop or cell phone. And for the latter, newer security systems don't require a landline anymore, and are often less expensive for monthly monitoring. (More on that in the very next subject discussing home security systems).

Eliminate that landline and save about $20 per month. Sometimes this is part of a package, but you can still save money by eliminating it. Can you guess how much *not* having a home phone (that thing that rings with strangers on the other end trying to sell you things you don't need? The one that interrupts you at dinnertime, yeah, that one.) can be worth????? $20 invested monthly =

10-year projected savings: $3,513

20-year projected savings: $10,750

30-year projected savings: $25,667

40-year projected savings: $56,410

*Say goodbye to the ring and hello to cha-ching!!!*


## Home Security

If you have home security monitoring, please shop it if you haven't already done so lately. Today, you can get wireless security including door cameras, monitored for as little as $15 per month. If you're paying $25 a month or more for security monitoring today, converting your monitoring system and saving that $10 per month could mean another nice addition to your retirement! (The small leaks keep coming!)

10-year investment savings: $1,757

20-year investment savings: $5,377

30-year investment savings: $12,838

40-year investment savings: $28,214

*Don't get robbed by your security company!!!*

## Insurance, (Auto)

Shop this around!!! If you have a decent driving record, there is a reliable company out there that would love to get your business. Let's make this easy; Do an internet search: 'compare auto insurance'. You'll get bombarded by companies and agents... And, yes, there will be forms to fill out, but your valuable time should be rewarded with a lower cost alternative!

If you happen to love your current insurer, there are also ways you can save with them. Among various potential areas for savings are the amount of your deductible, coverage amount, roadside assistance, rental vehicles and other categories. I have shopped this a few times and have been able to save close to $200 per year on two different occasions. I wasn't successful on the last call I made, and that's OK, as it means I've trimmed my expense to a low level.

Let's sidebar again for a moment. Companies are doing their best to be profitable. So should you! Just because someone sends you a quote doesn't mean it's exactly what you need. Take the time to shop around and carefully review your policies. End sidebar....

Saving and investing a $200 annual amount with an expected 7.5% annual growth??? Let's call it $15 invested per month:

Retirement Savings on $15 per month =

10-year projected savings: $2,635

20-year projected savings: $8,064

30-year projected savings: $19,252

40-year projected savings: $42,312

*Insure your future!!!*

Again, a reminder that you're not going to pay the same premiums every year on auto insurance. But once you begin saving that amount, (in this example, $200), even if your rate doesn't remain the same, you're going to do everything in your power to keep contributing every month and year, right?

## Insurance, Auto (Cont'd)

There are other ways to reduce your auto insurance. This one is subtle: If you like buying used cars, find and purchase a higher mileage vehicle! You'll not only save money on the car, but you will also experience a lower insurance premium.

The more money your car is worth, the higher the insurance premiums. Thus, if you like the look of an expensive car, find a higher mileage vehicle!

For instance, let's look at the Toyota Camry. The average monthly insurance premium for a 2016 Camry is estimated at $151.61 vs. a 2021 Camry premium at $183.69, or a difference of $32.08 per month.[37] Let's look at what happens when you save that money and invest just $32 monthly:

10-year projected savings = $5,619

20-year projected savings = $17,197

30-year projected savings = $41,061

40-year projected savings = $90,245

*Put a premium on saving and investing!!!*

The numbers become more interesting, (and even exciting) when you combine the savings on both the monthly payment and the insurance premium for your less expensive vehicle! When you add those together isn't the combined invested savings worth a serious

---

[37] Peter Carleton, "Toyota Camry Insurance Rates," Finder, July 21, 2021, https://www.finder.com/car-insurance/toyota-camry-insurance-rates

look? If you're ready to become an investor, making this subtle tweak in how you buy your vehicles could be a *life changer!*

Note that there are other factors that can help to reduce insurance premiums, such as how fast your car will go, and the size. Generally, the slower and smaller the car, the lower the insurance cost!

## Insurance (Bundle)

If you're getting your auto insurance from one company, and your homeowner's insurance from another, most companies offer up to a 25% discount by combining policies with one company.

Hopefully you're doing this already, but if not, BIG SAVINGS could be sitting in front of you... In the United States, full coverage car insurance costs an average of $2,014 per year, while minimum coverage is $622 per year.[38] Let's use a reasonable example of $1,200 per year. And for homeowners' insurance, the national average premium is **$1,428 per year**.[39] We'll average that at $1,200 annually as well, making a total of $2,400 spent per year for both, for this example.

Now that we have a basis for our example, a 25% discount off the $2,400 total equates to $600 annually, or $50 saved monthly. To get your actual potential savings, add your two premiums together and multiply by .25. Using our example, saving $50 monthly can give your retirement fund a more-than-solid boost:

10-year projected savings: $8,778

20-year projected savings: $26,869

---

[38] Shannon Martin, "Average Cost of Car Insurance in November, 2023," Bankrate.com, November 10, 2023, https://www.bankrate.com/insurance/car/average-cost-of-car-insurance/

[39] Shannon Martin, "Average Cost of Homeowners Insurance in November, 2023," Bankrate.com, November 10, 2023, https://www.bankrate.com/insurance/homeowners-insurance/homeowners-insurance-cost/

30-year projected savings: $64,153

40-year projected savings: $140,998

*This easy idea could make you a 'bundle'!!!*


## Insurance, (Homeowners)

If you currently own a home, take a moment and study your policy. Chances are good some of you have not reviewed this document. More than half of homeowners (56%) did not review their home insurance policy in the last year to see how much coverage they had. In fact, nearly 20% have never reviewed their policies.[40] For some, the policy was studied when the home was first purchased but not since, as it's usually paid right along with your mortgage. Out of sight, out of mind...

On one occasion, after paying my homeowners rate for more than 3 years, I finally sat down and studied the numbers. My insurance company was insuring me for much more than I needed to replace my house and contents!

With one phone call, a couple of emails and an e-signature, *I saved close to $700 annually.* Caveat emptor, and it was my oversight in not keeping up with my policy declarations. This is an example of exactly what we're attempting to accomplish here: We are finding leaks where we might be paying too much.

A $700 annual investment could be life-changing over the coming years. Let's assume you pursue this tactic and realize savings as well. We'll use a smaller, more attainable number. Let's suggest some of

---

[40] Pat Howard, "Majority of US homeowners may not have enough insurance to rebuild after a disaster," Policy Genius, February 22, 2023, https://www.policygenius.com/homeowners-insurance/home-insurance-inflation-survey-2023/#:~:text=Two%20in%20three%20%2868%25%29%20homeowners%20who%20reviewed%20their,coverages%2C%2015%25%20have%20none%2C%20and%2044%25%20aren%E2%80%99t%20sure.

you can find an approximate $240 annual savings or $20 monthly, which you now invest:

10-year projected savings: $3,513

20-year projected savings: $10,750

30-year projected savings: $25,667

We'll stop at 30 since that is the maximum length of traditional mortgages.

*Your home might be worth more to you than you think!!!*

## Insurance, (Life)

If you are married and/or have a family, do you know how much life insurance you need? If you own a home, what is the balance on your mortgage? You need to have *at least* that much life insurance. And then, how much cash will your spouse/family need to survive in the unlikely event of your death? Add those two items together, and any other details that pertain to your situation (debt, medical needs, future needs that you're aware of).

Let's say you signed up for a million-dollar life insurance policy a number of years ago, as that was the amount of coverage needed to cover your family. As your mortgage value decreases over the years, and hopefully as your wealth grows, you should not need to keep that policy at a full million, unless of course you choose to.

For instance, if you had a million-dollar policy, and if you find over the years that you have gained $200,000 equity in your home, and you have $100,000 in the bank or your retirement fund, you now might only need $700,000 in life insurance. Similarly, as you get older and your wealth builds, you may decide that your coverage doesn't need to be as high!

What does life insurance cost? 'For the average 35-year-old man, every $100,000 in term life insurance will cost $22.14.'[41] This number will rise with age or will be less if you are younger.

Let's suggest you purchased a half million-dollar policy when you got married and were 25. Great move… Well, now it's 15 years later, you're 35, and maybe you have gained $100,000 in home equity, and have $50,000 saved in your retirement fund. Thus, now you only need $350k in insurance to provide that $500k to your family… You have a choice: You can either have a surplus of insurance money available for your family, or you could save and invest some of that money by lowering your life insurance coverage.

This is NOT a suggestion or endorsement that you should lower your life insurance coverage. This is a recommendation to analyze it. You might find that you need more coverage! But if you decide that you're over-insured, you could create dollars suitable for saving and investing. And isn't investing in your retirement like the idea of life insurance? Both are done with the future in mind.

Take the time to investigate your coverage! Remember also as you calculate your life insurance needs that if you are currently working, your employer may already be providing a nice chunk of your insurance needs at little or no cost to you. This is often found among your company's medical benefits.

If you're able to lower your coverage by $100,000 and save nearly $20 monthly, you'll be able to add to your personal investment savings!

10-year projected savings: $3,513

20-year projected savings: $10,750

---

[41] "How Much Does a $100,000 Life Insurance Policy Cost," Profam, December 13, 2023, https://www.profam.com/100000-dollar-life-insurance/

30-year projected savings: $25,667

40-year projected savings: $56,410

Some of you could find you're able to save 2-3-4X that amount and still have the right coverage. That could be a game changer.

*Protect your life!!!*


## Insurance: (Home Title Protection)

Have you seen commercials about unscrupulous people stealing people's home titles, or taking out a loan against homes without the owner knowing about it? If so, you may have purchased home title protection insurance (this is different from actual home title insurance, which protects you from issues with your title that occurred before you bought your home).

Home title protection companies offer you a service (it's not really insurance, they don't cover your losses against fraud) that monitors your deed and informs you if there are any changes, such as someone unscrupulously changing your title information, billing address or trying to request a loan or make an inquiry on your title.

The typical cost for this insurance is about $14.99 per month or $180 per year. I have good news for anyone currently protecting their home and title with this option. Most counties have a free notification option that will AUTOMATICALLY alert you if anyone attempts to change anything having to do with your title.

If you're paying that $180 per year for peace of mind coverage, take the time to log on to your county's website or email your county recorder's office and ask them how you can be alerted to any inquiry on your title. There may be a link on their website to turn this feature on.

What would saving $180 annually look like? Saving $15 per month:

10-year projected savings: $2,635

20-year projected savings: $8,064

30-year projected savings: $19,252

40-year projected savings: $42,312

*Your title is worthy!*


## Internet

Your home internet provider can be bundled with other services, or you may be paying for it separately. Try calling your provider and let them know you enjoy their service but are shopping around, as you need to reduce your bill and have seen lower offers advertised. They may offer you a one-year deal with a monthly discount. You can repeat the process next year or shop for better rates!

I easily saved $10 per month last time I did so. Saving yet another $10 can provide you with an additional projected:

10-year investment savings: $1,757

20-year investment savings: $5,377

30-year investment savings: $12,838

40-year investment savings: $28,214

*'Make the internet a portfolio asset!!!'*


## Internet, cont'd: Online Orders, (all of them)

If you're not doing this, for every single order you place online, before you click 'Place Order,' *STOP!!* Minimize that order on your screen, and if you're ordering a pair of capris from New Jersey, or a new jersey from Capri, search for their coupons'. If you're ordering a pizza from 'Jerry's Tacos' or tacos from 'Jerry's Pizza', search the company out and you'll often find a discount allowing you to pay less.

I won't put a dollar amount on this because everyone's online shopping habits are different, but you will save money. For our family, here's one example that is real; We have done this with a famous pizza company, and we have saved 25% - 30% on every purchase for many years.

That practice has saved us at least $15/month, or $180 a year. You'll see what that looks like invested below.

So, you can pay what they say it costs, or you can take 10-20 more seconds and search for their 'coupons' or 'promo codes' on the internet. You'll often find money you can keep in your pocket. Then, you must be sure to dedicate those saved dollars to your savings account to help pay that retirement bill!

Saving $15 per month by searching for online coupons can equate to:

10-year projected savings: $2,635

20-year projected savings: $8,064

30-year projected savings: $19,252

40-year projected savings: $42,312

*Get your piece of the pie!!!*

"Really, that much can be earned just by taking the time to add a coupon code?" Yes, really. But only when you invest your savings!


## Internet Selling

Some of you are skilled at getting the most out of the Internet. There is an avenue to saving more money on your online orders that many are undertaking. My daughter taught me this one: Become an internet seller! You can pay yourself and receive between 2 - 8% commission back just for being in the middle of the sale of the item that you purchased for yourself!

Here's how that would work: Every time you find something you would like to purchase online, rather than simply purchasing it directly, use your own small business internet store, (a website that you have created using perhaps Shopify, Squarespace, etc.), and purchase the product through your store's link. And BINGO! You will receive the commission from the company that you just purchased from.

Most internet sellers market their business and earn money from family, friends, and anyone who internet shops. They can enter your online store or as an alternative, every time they find something they want to buy, they'll contact you first to send them a link to your store, and you can be the dealer and get paid for being involved in those sales as well!

So, how much do you buy online monthly? Is it a hundred or a couple hundred dollars? Earning a 5% average commission from $200 in monthly purchases gets us right back to that magical, seemingly small $10 monthly savings. Next step is to invest that $10!

10-year investment savings: $1,757

20-year investment savings: $5,377

30-year investment savings: $12,838

40-year investment savings: $28,214

*Get paid to shop!!!*


## Job Relocation

While this idea is rare in that it carries an exception that would require a unique sacrifice, the concept and method of saving and investing to find your pot of gold is consistent. And this pot can be life-changing! Let's go:

Let's suggest for this example that Jane is earning somewhere around the median income in the USA, about $70,000 per year.[42]  Not rich, but doing pretty darn good and working her way up, right?  And finally, let's surmise that she's living in a state that charges a state income tax.  Her state thus charges Jane a 6% tax for the awesome privilege to live there, and she may have paid about $4,200 in state tax last year.

If Jane were to live in Florida, Tennessee, Texas, or any of the other 6 United States with zero state income tax?  (Yes, there are states that don't tax your income to live there….)  She just saved that $4,200, or part of it, and in effect, earned that much more than the lady in the other state who was 'earning' the same amount.

Before moving on, let's acknowledge that zero income tax states collect their revenue from other sources, such as toll roads, tourism, higher gasoline or property taxes, utilities charges, federal subsidies and many, many other areas.  They will get some of your money, but you can also control and avoid much of that.

So, let's just use $3,000 of Jane's potential annual savings, rather than the $4,200 'pay raise' that would appear instantly in her paycheck by moving to a zero-tax state.

Here's where Jane creates money and savings; She takes a similar paying job in a 'no state tax' state.  Perhaps Jane checks with her company, and they allow her to transfer to another locale, or she loads up the moving van and just goes for it….

Jane now has up to $4,200 more in her pocket annually, which we'll estimate to be a net $3,000 gain.  She now begins *investing that $3,000 'pay raise'.*  $3,000 per year divided by 12 months equals $250 per month.  As soon as she begins seeing her 'pay raise', Jane

---

[42] Jessica Semega and Melissa Kollar, "Income in the United States: 2021," United States Census Bureau, September 13,2022, https://www.census.gov/library/publications/2022/demo/p60-276.html

has the $250 monthly surplus automatically transferred from her bank into her investment account.

What will that amount mean to the bottom line in her retirement account?

10-year projected savings: $43,883

20-year projected savings: $134,326

30-year projected savings: $320,731

40-year projected savings: $704,917

*Untax yourself for a wealthy future!!!*

Before we move on, **let's make *INSTANT MILLIONAIRES* and fulfill retirement dreams right now!** (Lotto victory is not necessary!).

Using the state tax savings concept above, what if you're earning more than twice the national average income, or let's say $150,000 per year? That's pretty darn good! But, like half of America, you're not able to save much of that. You have mortgaged a big new house for your growing family, and you and your spouse both drive beautiful new financed cars full of upgrades.

Life is great! You are 20-30-40 something and living during an exciting time! You may not have begun focusing on your retirement just yet and your spending habits might keep you from being able to save. You're still young and there's plenty of time for that later, right? Remember, nearly half of us spend all of what we earn, regardless of income!

Continuing with the same situation as above, if you also live in a state that charges that 6% state tax, and earn $150,000 annually, *and if you found a similar job in a state that doesn't charge you that state tax,* would you like to venture a guess at what that 6% savings could be worth if you invested it annually for the next 30 years?

You sir / madam could someday join the **millionaire club.** *That big treasure chest could be waiting for you!!!!*

Just to clarify, if you invested your *entire* 6% tax savings ($9,000 annually, or $750 monthly) into your new retirement fund annually at an average 7.5% growth rate, you could have a projected **$962,175** in your bank in 30 years. In fact, regardless of your timeframe, this one could change your game in a big way.

Question, and I know you probably love your state: *But do you love it more than a million bucks?*

What's the key? **Same as the last nice lady, you enhanced your 'take home pay' without changing your earnings, and you immediately invested your newly found money and watched as your contributions grew quickly.** Each category below represents life-changing numbers!

10-year projected savings: $131,645

20-year projected savings: $402,969

30-year projected savings: $962,175

40-year projected savings: $2,114,716

Did your eyes happen to see that 40-year number? Wow, just wow... How about the 10-year estimate? If you're playing catch-up and looking for ideas...

As mentioned earlier, this opportunity is an outlier in that it is one of just a few that might require you to make a significant change. For the right person and situation, this one change can be life-altering!

-----*INTERMEZZO*-----

Let's take a break and review your worksheet! This can be an exciting moment. Hopefully you have found a number of ideas for consideration, and you've added your monthly and total savings as you've progressed.

Have you found $50 that you can save every month? $100? $200? $500? Did you get to a thousand? No matter where you currently stand, so long as you have made progress, you are on your way to being an investor!

There may be some who have already calculated that they can surpass their initial goal. Congratulations are in order! (And let's reset that goal!) For those who aren't there yet, *fear not!* As they say, *'Wait, there's MORE!'* A lot more.

Let's talk for a moment about saving money this year, and then assume we can keep it going over the next 10-20-30-40 years as an investment. None of your savings may be permanent!

What we *are* working to make permanent is the habit of saving within you. Saving creates a repeatable pattern as you ***think of your monthly savings like it's another bill.***

It's of utmost importance that you keep putting that monthly investment toward your retirement.

Have you noticed that most of the projected savings amounts you've seen thus far begin in the THOUSANDS OF DOLLARS? Sometimes *TENS OF THOUSANDS*, and sometimes *HUNDREDS OF THOUSANDS!*

Ok, break's over, let's get back to it and continue to upgrade that future!

# Chapter 17:
## The Savings Opportunities
## L Through Z

### Lawncare

This one is for those of you who contract out your yard work. I've also done that. Then I got a push mower. Then, with the approval of the President of my family, as well as my neighbor Mandy, the Queen Mum of my friend Gary, an agreement was struck. We got rid of our push lawn mowers, and we went halves on a new riding mower. (It had a cup holder, we couldn't resist). That mower cost us $1,800. Over the next 10 years, including the cost of the mower, we each saved close to $1,000 annually.

Aside from ensuring there was something cold in that cup holder, we were involved in an activity that included cardio exercise, weight loss, and a free tanning bed to boot, since we were compelled to be outdoors. We were trimming hedges, edging, and weed whacking, rather than snoozing in our lazy boys while paying someone else to take care of our green growth outdoors.

If you're currently paying someone to cut your grass, this idea could make your world a bit greener. If you're able to save $1,000 annually by doing it yourself, well… I'll use the low end: $1,000 = $83.33 per month. When I was contracting our lawn service out, I was paying $110 per month, or $1,360 annually with a yard that was a little under ¾ of an acre. After purchasing the rider, and considering gasoline, oil changes and mower repairs, saving $1,000 annually or $83 per month sounds reasonable.

Are you ready? And don't forget the side-benefits…. you might drop a few pounds and find yourself with an irresistible tan as you manage your lawn…. (Favor to ask: Don't wear sandals if you're taking this one on). $83 monthly:

RETIREMENT SAVINGS AT 7.5% =

10-year projected savings: $14,571

20-year projected savings: $44,599

30-year projected savings: $106,488

40-year projected savings: $234,045

*You came, you mowed, you kicked grass!!!*


## Lawn Fertilization

Another easy spot to save some money!  If you have a lawn and you've decided you're going to be taking care of it, why not buy a spreader and fertilize it, too?  Take charge of your great outdoors!

While this is not a monthly service, it may be charged monthly and can be included with lawn service.  Typically, 2x fertilizations per year at an average cost of about $60 per treatment = $120 farmed out annually.  Depending on where you live, you might also need a weed killing application sometime during the summer, at a similar cost.  Let's use a cost estimate of $180 per year to pay for fertilization service.

You can buy fertilizer and weed killer for about $20 per application for the average size lawn.  You might save $100 per year after also buying your $20 spreader.  Let's estimate $40 saved per application, $120 annually, or $10 per month.  This is quick work, and it gets you outdoors and even this little task can add a big bundle of Jeffersons to your future if you do it yourself:

10-year investment savings: $1,757

20-year investment savings: $5,377

30-year investment savings: $12,838

40-year investment savings: $28,214

*Fertilize your green future!*


119

It seems hard to believe that fertilizing your own lawn for the next 40 years, rather than farming it out to a lawn service, could net you another $28,214, but it's possible if you invest what you save, putting that $10 into a fund every month!

## Maid Service

Many of us know friends or acquaintances who are not wealthy who have paid for or are currently paying someone to clean their house once or twice per month.

You'll have to consider if avoiding vacuuming, mopping, and dusting is truly worth the chest of treasure and wealth you'll see below.

If you're paying someone $100 twice a month…. Prepare to be blown away at your good fortune if you decide to knock this service out of your monthly expenses. $200 monthly savings =

10-year projected savings: $35,107

20-year projected savings: $107,461

30-year projected savings: $256,586

40-year projected savings: $563,938

I'll also provide a $100 monthly estimate in case you're paying near that amount monthly:

10-year projected savings: $17,555

20-year projected savings: $53,733

30-year projected savings: $128,298

40-year projected savings: $281,978

If you are currently paying for this service, cleaning your own house, and investing the savings monthly could be one of the easier paths to your wealthy retirement.

*Whistle while you work!!  Clean up later by cleaning up now!!!*

Lawn Care and Maid Service can be looked at together for a reason, thus I have put them together, slightly out of alphabetical order.  They are closely related *optional* services.  It's a luxury to come home from work and not have to spend time on the weekend mowing or cleaning.  But it might also be considered a luxury to add a half million dollars or more to your bank!

In your opinion, which is the better use of that money?  Remember, there's no wrong answer!

Put those two services together and look at the number of years that apply to your situation.  If you're in the '40 more years of work until you retire' category, you'll see that you could be looking at *over $800,000 WAITING IN YOUR RETIREMENT FUND JUST BY MAKING THE DECISION TO TAKE CARE OF THESE 2 SERVICES YOURSELF*, and by investing that money that you would have spent.

If you're in the 'working 30 more years' category, you're approaching *$400 GRAND!*

If you're in the 20-year group, *that still could be over $150K!*

*And if you're in the 10-year category, every dollar counts to get your nest egg caught up.  This opportunity could provide you with over $50,000 saved over the next 10 years!!!*


## Lunch at Work: Sub Shop/Burger Joint

During our workday, when lunchtime comes around, many of us eat out.  However, for those of you who hit a restaurant just because you can afford it, or even if you are part of a group that goes out together, how would *you* like to upgrade your future???

That $8 chicken sandwich or sub?  Change it to a homemade meal you create and pack right in your very own gourmet kitchen!  Ever wonder how much difference that could make in your future?

Let's estimate that you can make your own lunch for about $2.00. (2 pieces of your favorite bread, premium deli meats, chips (maybe you bought 2 for the price of 1), pickles, a baggie, and a bottle of water (note, eating this could also help trim a few pounds vs. the burger or submarine sandwich, so there might be a good synergy there). Better yet, put tap water in a cooled tumbler...But let's go with the bottled water or a soda at 30 to 40 cents each.

If the numbers above are realistic, you might be able to save somewhere around $6 per day. If you total about twenty workdays a month, that's around $120 each month that you could now save.

If this seems too painful and too much of a sacrifice, you could split the difference and just eat out 2 or 3 times a week, just on Monday and Friday for instance, and still save $50 a month or more.

Using the full amount, just have a look at the 10-year number. You could have a projected $21,615 in your pocket over the next 10 years!! $120 savings per month invested:

10-year projected savings = $21,065

20-year projected savings = $64,479

30-year projected savings = $153,955

40-year projected savings = $338,370

*Eat your way to riches!!!*


## Military and Veterans Discounts

If you have served your country honorably, by signing up for military related discounts at ecommerce sites that focus on military members, and by shopping at the many businesses that honor your service, you can save money, receive free event tickets and more.

As a veteran, I am frequently sent offers for free tickets to numerous sporting and concert events and other performances in my area. I am also notified of discounts on merchandise. Do your own search for 'military discounts.' There are hundreds of opportunities for military/veterans.

How much would you say you spend annually at Home Depot or Lowe's? Or Advance Auto Parts, or Michael's, or Old Navy or Kohl's or GameStop, or… the list goes on and on! Let's pretend you average spending $100 monthly at these stores combined. There's another of those $10 monthly savings that will *add up.* Your military service will typically garner you about 10% in discounts when shopping at any stores that honor and recognize your service. There are numerous businesses that offer you savings. Taking advantage of these discounts at an estimated at $10 monthly savings can be worth:

10-year investment savings: $1,757

20-year investment savings: $5,377

30-year investment savings: $12,838

40-year investment savings: $28,214

*Your service continues to provide value!!!*


## Mortgage Refinance

If you own a home, depending on when you purchased it and what the rate was, you may be able to save money every month, potentially a LARGE SUM. You've seen the commercials, and the savings can be real. If you're currently paying, for instance, 7% on a $100,000 mortgage, by getting in on a lower 6% rate, you might be able to recoup a substantial $100 per month. What does that look like if you invest $100 for the next 10, 20 or 30 years (mortgages max out at 30)?

10-year projected savings: $17,555

20-year projected savings: $53,733

30-year projected savings: $128,298

*Interest-ed?*

## Mortgage Payment Insurance, (PMI)

For any homeowners, Private Mortgage Insurance sure seems like a nice privilege for the bank, doesn't it? When you purchase a house, 'Mortgage Insurance' is already included in your payment. But that's for you. PMI is another type of insurance to protect *the bank* in the event you default on your loan. And YOU get to pay that insurance! What a great gig!

Not everyone has to pay PMI. It is required for any home buyer who doesn't put down at least 20% on their home, and in certain other circumstances. What's the charge? Anywhere from ½ to 1 ½ percent of the cost of the house. So, for someone buying a $300,000 home with a minimal down payment, they'll need to pay for PMI, meaning an additional $150-450 per month could be added to their payment. That could mean paying thousands more per year! It's added to your payment, and you may not even notice or feel it, except for the fact that you don't have as much money.

The first bit of advice would be to NEVER pay PMI. Before you purchase your first home, have enough saved to put that 20% down. Note, if you are or were in the military, you may be eligible for a VA loan, which pays your PMI for you, a fantastic benefit and value!

Here are the potential savings if you avoided paying PMI on a less expensive house that cost $100,000. (1% = $1,000 annually for PMI, or $83.33 per month). (For a differently priced home, take the difference in your home cost and multiply it times the added value, i.e. if your house cost $300,000, multiply the numbers below x 3, and so-on). $83 invested monthly:

10-year projected savings: $14,571

20-year projected savings: $44,599

30-year projected savings: $106,488

Remember, this calculation is on a $100,000 home. Imagine the size of the investment savings if you're able to eliminate PMI on a larger palace!

Another note, if you are currently paying PMI, it should be temporary. Once you've made enough payments to get your equity above that 20% level, your PMI should be removed by the lender, and you can then begin investing those savings to give your retirement fund a *huge* boost! If you are close to that 20% number, consider packing your savings toward your home equity until you can eliminate PMI!

*PMI = Preventing Momentous Investments*

## One-Time Income Events, Invest your Income Tax Return and Garage Sale Income

If you often get a refund when completing your income taxes, or if you happen to have a garage sale occasionally, you should consider investing your profit rather than spending it. While it might not sound like much at the time, one-time investments can help to fill your treasure chest nicely. Below, a few potential amounts are listed as well as what they could be worth to you upon your retirement.

$250 one-time investment

   10-year projected savings = $515

   20-year projected savings = $1,062

   30-year projected savings = $2,189

   40-year projected savings = $4,511


$500 one-time investment

   10-year projected savings = $1,031

   20-year projected savings = $2,124

   30-year projected savings = $4,377

40-year projected savings = $9,022


$1,000 one-time investment

    10-year projected savings = $2,061

    20-year projected savings = $4,248

    30-year projected savings = $8,755

    40-year projected savings = $18,044


$5,000 one-time investment

    10-year projected savings = $10,305

    20-year projected savings = $21,239

    30-year projected savings = $43,775

    40-year projected savings = $90,221

Think for a moment about what investing the profits from having a garage sale or your tax return *each year* could do for you!  In some cases, **this strategy alone could fund a significant portion of retirement.**  Here's one example:  $1,000 invested once per year for each of the next 40 years at a 7.5% annual return rate would result in **$227,275** overflowing from your investment treasure chest!  The math is excellent: You deposit $40,000, you withdraw $227,275!

*Gotta love that kinda math!!!*


## Pizza, One More Time

Since everyone loves talking about Pizza, I had to bring it up again.  If you are one of those who love to order pizza delivery (that's everyone, correct?) here is a money saving opp for you:  Rather than calling the pizza company, reach into your freezer and pull out one of those $7 frozen pizzas (that perhaps you bought when there was a two-for-one special, even better!). You avoid paying 2-3-4 times the price for having it delivered. Let's say you eat pizza twice per month. You could save about $10 on each pizza or $20 monthly.

By cooking your own, you might even be able to sink your teeth into that hot piece of heaven before it would have been delivered... What could baking your own pizzas add to your retirement at $20 per month? If you make this tiny change in your life and direct those savings to your investment account, WOW. No joke, this one could enhance some futures. Run the numbers on your own pizza passion. For this example, $20 saved monthly =

10-year projected savings: $3,513

20-year projected savings: $10,750

30-year projected savings: $25,667

40-year projected savings: $56,410

*Bake up a new life!!!*


## Prescriptions

Do you think all prescriptions are the same price, no matter where you buy them? Did you know that Ampicillin might be WAY less expensive at Target than it is at Walgreens, or Apriso might be ½ the cost at Publix compared to CVS. Humalog might be priced much lower at Walgreens than it is at Wegmans. This is regional, so you MUST check. It's very easy to analyze online, simply do a search of 'prescription prices.'

There are also Prescription discount opportunities with third parties such as GoodRX and SingleCare which will help you find the lowest cost near you and offer huge savings with no obligation. Whether you have insurance or not, prescription discounts can work for you if you don't mind going to additional locations other than where you normally pick up your meds.

The savings could be massive to you, up to hundreds for each prescription depending on your medical needs. If you have a regular prescription that you will always need, and if you have not shopped the price around recently, please take the time, it could be worth thousands of dollars over your lifetime!

*A prescription for a cozier future!!!*


## Rent

The cost of rent has been skyrocketing over the past few years, creating a hardship for many. The trend of young adults moving back in with their parents, especially since the pandemic, is real.[43] And for both the parents and their children, this may not be a perfect situation.

For those who have been fortunate enough to be able to continue renting, the good news is that there are *numerous* opportunities for additional saving. Consider:

-If you love where you live and have no plans to relocate, try offering to sign an extension for multiple years on your lease at a reduced rate. You could negotiate, for instance, a 5% discount, significant dollars.

-If you are handy, you can offer to upgrade, paint or repair items in need in exchange for lower rent or a credit. Your landlord would prefer that arrangement to contracting a full-price job.

-Rent your parking space. Some facilities provide covered or nearby parking for tenants while guests and extra vehicles

---

[43] Claire Murishima, "Gen Zers and millennials are moving back in with their parents in record numbers," NPR, December 11, 2022, https://www.npr.org/2022/12/11/1139330863/genz-millennials-living-parents#:~:text=Many%20Gen%20Zers%20and%20millennials,to%20a%202022%20LendingTree%20survey.

park outside or elsewhere. You may be able to rent your space depending on your location.

-If you have room, consider adding a roommate. This could cut your rent in half or more, completely altering your monthly finances!

-Move! There is always a lower priced rental option available. Determine the magic number that would make the move worth it to you, and shop around! If you're struggling to pay the bills now and can save $200-$300 or more monthly, your financial situation can become more comfortable.

-Finally, there is nothing wrong or unusual with negotiating with the owner/landlord when lease renewal time comes around. Even working $20 off your monthly rent is another $240 in your pocket annually. It should be worth it to your landlord rather than risk having the apartment unrented for even a month.

If you're renting and willing to attempt a negotiation with your landlord, let's suggest that you find a way to cut your monthly rent by $20 the next time your lease comes around.

10-year projected savings: $3,513

20-year projected savings: $10,750

30-year projected savings: $25,667

40-year projected savings: $56,410

(Quick note; the chances of you saving $20 per month off the rent for the next 40 years are less than remote, however once you begin adding that amount to your auto deposit, you should scratch and claw to keep that money going toward your future every month, growing. It's only $20! Reducing the rent was just the catalyst!)

*Smaller payment = larger portfolio!!!*

## Restaurants

Where do you fit in the research below? '7.19% eat out an average of four days per week.' 'Next up, 15.65% eat out three days per week.' '25.08% eat out two days per week.' 'A whopping 44.25% of voters said they eat out just one day per week.'[44]

Once you've gotten into the proper line above, when you eat out, do you inevitably order an appetizer? If so, that might cost an average of $12-$15. And don't forget the tip. At 20%, that's another $2-$3. Let's value the appy at $15…

Has anyone out there ever had the thought at any time in their life that eliminating eating appetizers could create a sizable fortune in their future?

Try this! Go out and have a blast as usual, without ordering the hors d'oeuvre! Ask your waiter to bring you some bread instead….

Let's use a reasonable two times out per month with a savings of $15 per meal, or $30 per month that can be saved.

10-year projected savings: $5,268

20-year projected savings: $16,123

30-year projected savings: $38,495

40-year projected savings: $84,606

*Pass on the appy, make tomorrow more happy!!!*

---

[44] Autumn Swiers, "New Survey Shows How Often People Typically Eat Out," Tasting Table, October 7, 2022, https://www.tastingtable.com/912246/new-survey-shows-how-often-people-typically-eat-out/

## Restaurants, Frequency

How often do *you* eat out? Twice a week? Six times a month? And what would you estimate is the average cost per trip out? $25? $50? $100? More? Ever analyzed it?

What if you considered that by reducing the number of times you eat out per month by just one, you could have a comfortable safe deposit box filled with gold bullion waiting for you?

Do this: If you charge your meals, look back over the past 3 months credit card statements and count the number of times you dined out. Also write down the amounts you spent. Divide that number by three to get your monthly average.

Now, make your own decision to cut that average monthly amount by $50 or $100 per month. (Or even $20, it'll make a difference!) It's not like you're cutting out one of life's enjoyments, you're just reducing it by one! For this you'll have to set a budget and keep a record. If you're serious about converting restaurant dollars into retirement treasure, and you're able to save $100 per month, here's what that can do for your future:

10-year projected savings: $17,555

20-year projected savings: $53,733

30-year projected savings: $128,298

40-year projected savings: $281,978

The numbers above are not a joke! Remember, you're saving and investing that $100 amount religiously for the next 10, 20, 30, or 40 years, just like paying a bill.

*Increase your appetite for a satisfying future!!!*

## Roadside Assistance:

If there is one place in your bills that I could pick to guess where some of you are double paying for a service, it would be here. Do you have roadside assistance coverage such as AAA? Now, take a quick look at your auto insurance policy. There's a chance this is already covered. (Or maybe I was the only one....)

Other services such as purchasing extended warranty on your vehicle also add this coverage. If you're able to eliminate this double payment, you can save another $125 a year or so. I did! Another $10 saved per month!

10-year investment savings: $1,757

20-year investment savings: $5,377

30-year investment savings: $12,838

40-year investment savings: $28,214 (Wow)

*Seeing double? Save instead!!!*


## Satellite Radio

If you have Satellite radio in your vehicle, which plan are you paying for? If it's the top tier plan, you have the option to save up to $10 dollars monthly by dropping to fewer channels. Check the channel listing and see if you might be able to save $5-10 monthly.

This little decision can contribute to something beautiful in the future. Here is another opportunity to save $10 monthly:

10-year investment savings: $1,757

20-year investment savings: $5,377

30-year investment savings: $12,838

40-year investment savings: $28,214

*Are you serious???*

## Swimming Pool

Ah, swimming pools. Yes, we all want to own one, and many of us take them on. And they are *FUN, and BEAUTIFUL and TROPICAL!*

There is an old saying for pools, boats, and a select few other things in life: The happiest 2 days are the day you bought them, and the day you sold them. Pools and boats are spectacular, but with them comes much maintenance!

We had a chlorine pool, and my local pool service company offered 2 options; regulate the alkalinity/acidity of the pool, (cost was $90 per month and they stopped by weekly), or they could add cleaning the pool each week when they came by, ($150 per month for both services).

As I traveled a bit in my job, the alkalinity was one thing that I decided I would not be home enough to care for responsibly. But I did clean the pool myself. So, in my case, I was 'kind of' saving $60 per month.

If you own a chlorine pool (saltwater pools are much less expensive to care for) and farm out the work, many of you have an opportunity. If you want to save up to **$1,000 per year**, you can maintain a pool yourself.[45] It will take a little education as well as purchasing your own supplies. (My mother took stellar care of her own pool).

Rather than using the $1,000 savings suggested above, let's go with a slightly more reasonable $900, or a savings of $75 per month:

10-year projected savings: $13,166

20-year projected savings: $40,301

---

[45] Mizuki Hisaka, "How Much Does Swimming Pool Maintenance Cost? (2023 Data)," Angi, April 20, 2023, https://www.angi.com/articles/how-much-does-it-cost-maintain-swimming-pool.htm

30-year projected savings: $96,225

40-year projected savings: $211,488

Sometimes the numbers seem a little outrageous: "Am I *really* going to save over $200,000 just by taking care of my own pool? Give me a break!!!" Well, if you plan to have a pool all of your adult life, if you take care of a pool over the next 40 years and if you invest the savings ($75 per month) that you would have paid to have it done for you, and if your investments earn an average of 7.5%, then ...............YES!

*Per Ben Franklin, "When the well's dry, we know the worth of water."*


## TV: Cable, Satellite, Streaming

TV is a quickly evolving service and there seem to be new options coming every month. If you have cable TV and currently have premium channels, such as HBO, Starz or Showtime, how critical is that for you? If your premium channel is costing you just $15 per month, and you decide you can do without it:

10-year projected savings: $2,635

20-year projected savings: $8,064

30-year projected savings: $19,252

40-year projected savings: $42,312

After seeing these projections, is your premium channel still critical? It's fine if it is, by the way!

Next question: Do you have the 400-channel package, or the 300 or the 200? Whatever your answer is, step it down and see if you can live with the change. Look at your channel guide and consider knocking this package down a level, and see if it makes your life miserable, or if you can survive. You might find that it's worth it to say goodbye to one or two channels you like. $15 *more* saved:

10-year projected savings: $2,635

20-year projected savings: $8,064

30-year projected savings: $19,252

40-year projected savings: $42,312

Not leaving TV yet. If you have cable TV, cable receiver boxes can be important, too. You can typically get standard cable channels without the cable boxes. You may be able to connect your coax cable directly from the wall right into your TV connection, and you will have to do a channel scan to get your TV to recognize the channels. That has worked for me on one occasion and did not work on another. If you do this, you won't get the premium channels on those TV's. Your cable company would LOVE for you to have a receiver in all rooms. These boxes cost an average of $7 to $13 per month.

If you cut just two of them out of your household and still not consider it a hardship, here's what that savings would look like if you saved an average of, let's estimate, $20 per month:

10-year projected savings: $3,513

20-year projected savings: $10,750

30-year projected savings: $25,667

40-year projected savings: $56,410

A note about TV: It's safe to say that 40 years from now, (or even 6 months), TV will look a lot different. Streaming is today's hot commodity, and there will be new technology around the corner and in the coming years… this $20 savings might not be around forever… There will be another option in place of cable or satellite, and it will no doubt cost money, and you will then of course be looking for and finding ways to re-save that $20…. or more.

Another idea to help save monthly; There are other low-cost alternatives to cable and satellite, such as using a Firestick to get IPTV, which can cut your bill to a *small fraction* of what you are currently paying. If your current plan is oppressive to your situation and you want or need to cut your costs and save, this option offers big savings. Please consider it!

*Watch your net worth grow while you watch TV!!!*

## Water/Sewer

Water and sewer can be surprisingly expensive utilities. While it's difficult to quantify, we all know that reducing your water consumption will save you money. That can also reduce your sewer costs.

Ever wonder how much water we consume? 'The average American uses 82 gallons of water daily, costing the average family $1,100 annually, the Environmental Protection Agency (EPA) reports. And because the average family wastes 180 gallons of water per week, according to the EPA, there's lots of opportunity to save.'[46]

If you water your lawn, try reducing your timer by a few minutes and see if your grass still responds well. Turn the water off while you're brushing your teeth. Don't let it run for 5 minutes before you step into the shower. Don't leave the water running while you rinse the dishes. Try the quick cycle with clothes washing and your dishwasher to see if they meet your clean test. If your plumbing is outdated, new fixtures will save water. Newer appliances will also be more efficient.

The average water bill in the United States is $72.93 a month for a family of four using 100 gallons of water per day per person.[47]

---

[46] Karen Axelton, "9 Ways to Reduce Your Water Bill," Experian, July 25, 2022, https://www.experian.com/blogs/ask-experian/how-to-lower-water-bill/

[47] Laura Mueller, "How Much Is The Average Water Bill?" Moving.com, July 8, 2020, https://www.moving.com/tips/12-ways-to-lower-your-water-bill/#:~:text=As%20of%202019%2C%20the%20average,%2472.93%E2%80%94or%20%24875.16%20a%20year.

While water and sewer plans differ from region to region, if you're willing to take better care of your water usage, it's not unreasonable to suggest that you could reduce your average cost by 10% per month. Run your own test and analyze your numbers. If you invest the miniscule projected $7 monthly, look what it can become:

10-year projected savings: $1,231

20-year projected savings: $3,765

30-year projected savings: $8,989

40-year projected savings: $19,755

*Drip, drip, drip....*


## *CONGRATULATIONS, THIS CONCLUDES THE SAVINGS EXERCISE!*

The list of potential items we each consume is *limitless.* The list you just reviewed was long but does not cover every possibility with respect to your spending. **What other ideas can you add?** You can no doubt produce more ways to save based on your own spending habits and hobbies.

You are challenged to meditate for 5 minutes and come up with at least 1 or 2 additional ideas of your own. We're all about what *you* spend money on, how you spend it, and how you can save it!

Know that any ideas that you produce may be able to help others to improve their investing future. I welcome those ideas, please visit us at findyourhiddentreasurechest.com and share your ideas on our blog! Thank you in advance for any helpful input!

Below are a few more random saving ideas.

Hair. Ladies should use a discount hair salon from now on.... And that demonstrates why I'm not a comedian. Never, ever, under any circumstances suggest this or interfere with hair care. The same applies to shoes. Just look away and try to think of puppies or ice cream with sprinkles on top.

And you should know not to mess with your man's sports cards, video games, cigars, or beer! What we love says a lot about us, doesn't it? And please feel free to substitute for any gender specificity.

More real savings opportunities:

School supplies. Don't wait until the week before school starts! A little planning ahead can pay off. Buy as many of your supplies for next year as you can during the 2$^{nd}$ month of the semester, after everyone has finally bought what they need, and when the stores have left over inventory to dump. If you normally spend $100 on annual supplies and can save $25, why wouldn't you?

The same concept applies to Xmas lights and decorations. You can buy these items for as low as ten cents on the dollar in January!! Ditto for shopping for Halloween decorations in November and for other holidays after the fact.

Add your own ideas to your worksheet and include them in your savings plan!

*This should be an invigorating time.* Now that we've completed the savings exercise, we have just a couple of actions that need attention before our new financial plans are in place!

# Chapter 18:
# Act Now: Transform Your Savings From Concept To Reality

*"This chapter is monumental!"*

Congratulations on selecting the ideas and opportunities to cut your expenses and save money. You have a form full of savings ideas that you're about to bring back home! You've identified your chest of treasure and should be excited at the possibility of what it can mean to the trajectory of your future.

*While you can see that treasure, you can't count it yet. It is still just out of your reach...* To be able to quantify those bricks of gold bullion, or the jewels, or to feel the stacks of currency in your hands someday, it's time to act!

Now is the time when you **convert those savings from being ideas on your worksheet into a more valuable kind of paper, the green paper with famous faces on it...**

It is urgent that your new savings becomes the newest 'bill' that you'll pay, and something you pay Religiously, every month... This is the bill that remains yours! The magic happens once you have turned the estimated money on your worksheet into true savings.

**This task *now becomes your most important financial priority. Nothing else happens without your effort and action.***

You'll perform this process one opportunity at a time, by starting at the top of your list, and taking any and every necessary action to make your savings real.

For instance, let's say you've chosen to reduce your phone or cable TV bill. The time to call them is right now! (for example, "Hello cable company, I am calling to cancel my movie channels and review my account with you to reduce my bill.").

You'll act by doing whatever is required. More for instance:

- Cancel any services you're dropping.

- Log on or call to eliminate streaming options, unused phone apps, and other waste.

- Make changes around the house, adjust the thermostat, close off a room, adjust your sprinklers, etc.

- Buy the groceries you need to begin packing your lunch or brewing your own coffee.

- Review and call to modify your auto/life and home insurance policies.

- Buy dog clippers and make your first attempt at cutting your dog's hair.

*Whatever areas that you have chosen to change and save on.... Now is when you take every needed step to begin this transformation in your future.* This is very exciting, as **you get to witness new money coming back your way!**

These actions could take you minutes, hours, or longer. Take the time to formulate your strategy for each opportunity. This is not a time to rush. You're carefully re-arranging your future. Attack relentlessly until the task is done. It's only of the utmost importance!

This is also the exciting point where you should truly quantify your monthly savings amount. You may have selected saving $15 monthly on your cell phone bill. After your negotiation with your phone provider, you may have found that you'll instead save $10 or $18 or $33 monthly, your *actual* total.

Consider that you're about to reduce your monthly expenses. As you work to turn your imaginary dollars into *real money*, some of the companies that you are doing business with might want to negotiate or reverse your attempt to save by highlighting their value, quality, and other reasons you should stick with their service.

Keep in mind they're doing exactly what you are, looking for ways to cut costs and increase profitability! Do not be deterred from your decisions.

So, get ready, get set, and take the needed actions to make the savings you have discovered and chosen a reality.

*Tab this page and set the book down, and it is important that you don't return until you have made each of your necessary changes. You will need to know your true savings amount for the next task!*

*Put a SAVING MONEY, BE BACK SOON sign on your door and change your phone message to say, "SORRY I CAN'T TAKE YOUR CALL, WE'RE BUSY MAKING SOME CHANGES AROUND HERE."*

*TURN THE PAGE WHEN YOU RETURN*

Welcome back! You have spent time on hold, fought through online processes, altered a couple of things around the house, canceled or reduced unnecessary services, negotiated, studied the fine print in your bills, analyzed insurance policies, and more. Phew!

It won't happen today, but someday you may look back at this as a pivotal action taken in your life! You may have felt a rush once or twice as you witnessed new dollars adding up. You also instantly have better control of your finances and what you're spending!

You've taken care of the most time-consuming step! Now it's on to the final steps, which are the quick and easy tasks.

# Chapter 19:
# The Last Half Hour:
# Create Your Retirement Fund And Automatic Transfer

*"As the finish line comes into view, you may experience an adrenaline rush."*

This is it! Give yourself credit for working through the action stage of saving and improving your possibilities. Tomorrow should look and feel brighter!

We're now going to take the **final steps** and set up your <u>investment brokerage account for your retirement fund</u> as well as walk you through <u>automatically transferring</u> your newly found monthly savings from your paycheck/bank into that investment account. If you already have these steps in place, your job will be easy! Instructions follow for any scenario to ensure your investment account is in place.

**IF YOU HAVE DEBT**: For all participants who have loan or credit card balances, you know what you need to do. Your very first move will be to allocate ALL your new savings directly into an automatic monthly payment that will accelerate paying off your balance(s). Making this automatic will help to prevent you from spending the money and is crucial!

Even if this process takes 6 months, a year, or more, you are making a great move by eliminating your debt! An imaginary weight that's been on your shoulders will soon be removed.

Ensure you celebrate the occasion when you make that final payment, as becoming debt-free is a moment of euphoria! Bookmark this page, and once the payoff of your debt is complete, you can return to this book and section to begin your wealth building experience!

To create a brokerage account, you don't need to leave the house or visit anyone! (You can if you want to, by the way). We need to get that new money safely where it belongs, automatically every month, where it can begin to multiply over the coming years.

*THOSE OF YOU WHO WILL BE NEW TO THE INVESTING WORLD WILL BE ABLE TO SAY SOME MONUMENTAL AND PERHAPS LONG OVERDUE WORDS: "I AM AN INVESTOR." MARK THE DAY ON YOUR CALENDAR AND CELEBRATE IT EVERY YEAR!*

We're going to get your monthly savings safely building your treasure chest by automatically transferring them each month from your bank right into your brokerage account.

**The money in that account is still, and will always be yours,** available for emergencies and other important needs that could arise.

You may be wondering if there is a required cost or deposit to opening a brokerage account. The answer is 'NO!' This is a simple task. I recommend the online process because it's the one that has an 'Easy' button. Enrolling takes about 10-15 minutes, and they each have a quality phone app you can use whenever you feel the urge.

You might opt to visit your bank or a local brokerage and set your account up in person. You may prefer personal interaction, or you might have a friend or relative in the business that you wish to work with. That's all fine too!

IMPORTANT: If you happen to have other ideas for how you plan to invest (i.e. purchasing real estate, gold, collectibles, etc. as you save) you should still set up an investment account. You won't need to deposit any money into it if you don't want to. You might wish to later spread your portfolio out as it grows, and you can easily deposit any amount into the investment account where you can have the opportunity to grow and compound. Above all, ensure your money goes somewhere besides your wallet or purse each month!

Let's have a quick common-sense discussion on temptation, because as we know, it's everywhere; It could be easy to think to yourself, "Why don't I just slide this extra money into my pocket? I can always begin investing later when I feel like it!"

If you might have that thought, have a talk with your mirror: It should ask you, "What makes you think that if you don't change your behavior now that you'll suddenly do so later?" You've come so far and begun this process to become an investor. This is the time, not later. Finish the job!

Let's go! As has been mentioned, later in life you might think back and remember that opening your investment account was one of the best decisions you ever made. You'll be there in just a few minutes!!!

There are numerous scenarios below with respect to your **current** saving and investing situation. Scan each until you find the one that best describes and matches **you.** THEN SIMPLY FOLLOW THE INSTRUCTIONS:

1) **YOU ALREADY HAVE A 401K INVESTMENT PLAN**:

Log onto your 401k account and automatically adjust your monthly contribution upward by the amount of your new savings. Example: You earn $100,000 annually and currently contribute 3% of your income. You found $500 monthly to add to your savings. Adjust your contribution rate from 3% to 9%, ($500 per month equates to $6,000 annual increase, or adding 6%). You are DONE! Congratulations and enjoy watching your net worth grow rapidly!

**Note, if your added amount takes you over your maximum allowable contribution per year,** you will scroll below to #7, 'Opening your own investment account', and follow the instructions to begin depositing your excess savings into your own private account.

145

## 2) **YOU ALREADY HAVE A ROTH OR TRADITIONAL IRA**:

You may be self-employed, or you're working for a smaller company that doesn't offer a 401k plan, or perhaps you're simply contributing each year as you are able. Whether it's a Traditional IRA (before tax is deducted) or Roth IRA (after tax is deducted), you should be making one time, quarterly, or annual contributions. GREAT!

As of this writing, the maximum annual contribution allowed is $6,000 ($500 per month) up to 50 years of age, and $7,000 ($584 per month) if you're over 50. If you're not maxing or haven't maxed out your amount this year, (this may depend on what time of year you are reading this), you can add your new savings to your contribution until you are at the maximum.

If you aren't contributing regularly from your bank account, next, you're going to begin a monthly contribution of the amount of your newly found savings, or whatever portion of that savings you have chosen to invest.

Here's what you need to do: Log onto your IRA website, and then click on your 'Account.' Then click 'Deposits.' Then 'Contribution.' Enter the amount you're going to contribute monthly, and make sure you click on 'Monthly' where it asks for the 'Frequency.' And YOU ARE DONE.

ALREADY MAXING OUT YOUR IRA? IT'S TIME TO OPEN YOUR VERY OWN PERSONAL INVESTMENT ACCOUNT. Jump to # 7, 'Opening Your Own Investment Account'. What you might like about this account is your ability to easily move money, buy and sell stocks, bonds, mutual funds, metals etc. whenever you want. There is much freedom. Go to #7!

3) **YOU ALREADY HAVE YOUR OWN PRIVATE INVESTMENT ACCOUNT (not a 401k, or Roth or IRA)**

If you already have an automatic transfer being directed from your paycheck into your bank or online broker for your own investment purposes as you're able, (you might already have a separate 401k or IRA), you probably already know that you simply need to adjust your amount upwards to include your new monthly savings amount.

If you don't have an automatic transfer yet, (you're investing money as you're able to), login to your brokerage account, find and click on 'Contribution,' and enter the (new) amount you're going to contribute monthly, and make sure you click on 'Monthly' where it asks for the 'Frequency.'

If you don't already have a separate 401k or IRA plan, consider that it may be time to change your account designation to 'Retirement' or 'IRA' to take advantage of the SIGNIFICANT tax benefits available to you!

4) **YOU DON'T HAVE AN INVESTMENT OR RETIREMENT ACCOUNT AND YOUR PAYCHECK IS AUTOMATICALLY DEPOSITED INTO YOUR BANK**:

You have a TON of company if you're in this category. As discussed, nearly half of all working families DO NOT have any retirement savings. You're about to change that right now, though.

If your company offers a 401k and you haven't yet joined in on the fun, the time has come! Go to your company's retirement or 401k website. Create a login username and password and follow the instructions for how to set up your automatic monthly deduction. Call or chat with your company's retirement plan administrator if you need assistance.

If your company doesn't offer a 401k, you may be working for a smaller business with no retirement fund available. You will now open an IRA investment account through a Brokerage account, _or_ you will set up a new IRA brokerage account within your existing bank's checking and/or savings accounts. It's so easy, you still don't have to leave your house. (Again, you can if you want to...)

(Note, most banks have an investment branch, and most of these offer IRAs, although some of them only allow you to invest your money in lower interest paying CD's. If you prefer to keep everything at your bank, and you're good with safer investments with a little less topside growth potential, that's just fine, and well done!)

You can also use a credit union or savings and loan company, they'll be glad to have you saving your money with them, and they all offer IRA options.

If you opt for a new Brokerage account, select which company you prefer to do business with, (Schwab, Scottrade, Merrill Lynch, Fidelity, Goldman Sachs, etc.), and create a login and follow their prompts.

Once you have taken the steps to create your login info and set up your account, click on 'Retirement,' or 'IRA,' and 'Contribution.' Enter the amount you're going to contribute monthly, and make sure you click on 'Monthly' when it asks for the 'Frequency.'

You will be asked what account you will be sending the money from. You will need your Bank Routing Number, (the number on the bottom left of your personal checks), and your Account Number, (the number on the bottom right of your personal checks, except the last four numbers, which are your check number). Enter them and you are all set!

5) **YOU DON'T HAVE A RETIREMENT ACCOUNT AND GET A PAPER CHECK**:

Just like the folks in group #4, remember that nearly half of all working families DO NOT have any retirement savings. And you're about to change that right now and be in the *other* group, the one that is acting and investing in their future!

If you're given a physical paper paycheck, you may be working for a smaller company, job-hopping, doing occasional contracting or working part-time. Your situation will be simple! You will also open an IRA account with a brokerage firm. (You could also choose your bank, credit union, or savings and loan).

We'll assume you are physically depositing your check into your checking / savings account. If you currently cash your check, you will need to change your method and begin depositing it into your bank account, by either physically making this deposit at your bank, or by using an online deposit via your banking app, or by using apps such as Paypal, Venmo or Plaid.

Your new monthly savings amount *must* be transferred from your bank to your newly established IRA and investment brokerage account, which we will set up next.

Research and select a known investment company (Schwab, Scottrade, Merrill Lynch, Fidelity, Goldman Sachs, etc.). You can do a quick study of the pluses and minuses of each to see which appeals to you.

It takes about 10-15 minutes to create your login info and set up your investment account. Once completed, click on 'Retirement,' or 'IRA,' and 'Contribution.' Enter the amount you're going to contribute, and make sure you click on 'Monthly' where it asks for the 'Frequency.'

You will be asked what account you will be sending the money from; you will need your Bank Routing Number, (the number on the bottom left of your personal checks), and your Account Number, (the number on the bottom right of your personal checks, except the last 4 numbers, which are your check number). Enter them! Done!

## 6) **YOU ARE RECEIVING A DISABILITY OR SOCIAL SECURITY CHECK:**

If you are in this group, you may not be able to contribute to a Roth IRA due to income restrictions unless you are working. You're probably aware that there are income limits to how much money you can earn in addition to your disability payment, (currently $1,180 per month), and if you are working, some of that could be contributed to a Roth IRA.

In general, the easy route to begin with is to set up your own direct investment account. It's still your retirement account, but you won't see or feel the tax advantages that the 401K and IRA plans provide. But is that so bad? You have the right to build a golden nest egg like everyone else, and your time is now! So, your job is quite simple:

Your paycheck is either automatically deposited into your bank or is mailed to you and you then deposit it via your banking app, or other apps such as Paypal, Venmo or Plaid, into to your bank account. Maybe you physically deposit it.

What you'll need to do next is open a Brokerage account. Select which company you prefer to do business with, (Schwab, Scottrade, Merrill Lynch, Fidelity, Goldman Sachs, etc.), and create your login info and begin the process. Once you have taken the steps to set up your account, find and click on 'Deposit' and enter the amount you're going to contribute monthly, and make sure you click on 'Monthly' where it asks for the 'Frequency.'

You will be asked what account you will be sending the money from. You will need to provide your Bank Routing Number, (the number on the bottom left of your personal checks), and your Account Number, (the number on the bottom right of your personal checks, except the last four numbers, which are your check number). Enter them!

## 7) OPENING YOUR OWN PRIVATE INVESTMENT ACCOUNT:

It is simple to set up your own investment fund. Your paycheck has already been taxed and will not be taxed again. Your percentage gains from transactions on your deposits will only be taxed as you sell your investments at a profit, which is not a terrible thing. You would also be taxed on any distributions or dividends that your investments have paid you during that year.

To open your own private investment account, select which company you prefer to do business with, (Schwab, Scottrade, Merrill Lynch, Fidelity, Goldman Sachs, etc.), and login and follow the prompts.

Once you have taken the steps to create your login info and set up your account, click on either 'Brokerage and Trading' if this is not a qualified retirement account, (you either already have an IRA account, or you don't qualify for one), or 'Retirement' or 'IRA' if this is a qualified retirement account, (you don't have an IRA account). Next, click on 'Contribution.' Enter the amount you're going to contribute monthly, and make sure you click on 'Monthly' where it asks for the 'Frequency.'

You will be asked what account you will be sending the money from, you will need your Bank Routing Number, (the number on the bottom left of your personal checks), and your Account Number, (the number on the bottom right of your personal checks, except the last 4 numbers, which are your check number). Enter them!

You should be taking care of this final task right now! We are not messing around here or procrastinating. **To do *ANY* of it 'later' moves this duty down the priority list, where it can slowly fade away.** That would be a shame after coming this far.

Handcuff yourself to this book and get these accounts set up or changed to reflect your new savings amount! It should take you no more than a half hour, finish it NOW!

151

If you don't already have an account, completing this last act will be the finishing touch before allowing you to call yourself an investor, just like the rich!

It's time once again to **put this book down and don't come back until you've set up your brokerage account and your monthly bank transfers to the brokerage! See you in a half hour?**

**When you complete this task, turn the page!**

# Chapter 20:
## What Should I Invest In?

*"You've gotten smarter with your money, keep it going!"*

You now have a new retirement brokerage account with your name on it, (or more going into your existing account), and you have an automatic transfer that's going to direct funds from your bank to the new brokerage account every month. Your actions should bring you a high level of gratification. You've set your stage for a more comfortable and secure future.

Your first action should be to put on a pair of shades because your future is lookin' brighter! Next, you'll begin watching your funds get transferred monthly into your brokerage account.

At that point, you'll decide which investments to direct your funds toward. This is an exciting activity that can happen in a number of ways. Be confident that you're on the right track!

This book's goal is to help people build wealth. This book wants all participants to make thoughtful, careful investment decisions to give positive financial outcomes the best chance. With that said, below are some avenues for getting off on the right foot with your investment journey. As has been the case throughout, the choice on how to invest will be yours!

It can be a risky practice for others to suggest investing options for you. Taking recommendations or 'hot tips' from friends and relatives should probably be avoided. Most people would not want to feel responsible for another's loss. Even the best of intentions can go south, risking a relationship. Get off on the right foot:

Enlist The Services of a Financial Advisor

You may benefit most by using an Asset Manager or Financial Advisor (we'll use Advisor to mean any financial manager) and you can easily work with one at your new brokerage or bank. These money managers could be analogous to having a personal trainer. Sure, you can do it on your own, but with the help of a professional, your chances of proper direction and success are improved!

While an asset manager allocates and actively/passively manages your investment, the financial advisor takes a more expansive outlook on one's wealth and how to ensure that you get the most out of it and not purely to earn investment returns.[48]

If you're new to investing, it may be a 'best practice' to begin with an Advisor who can assist you. Call the toll-free number within your brokerage account or bank or visit your bank or local brokerage office. You can meet or they should be glad to work with you online or over the phone.

Your Advisor should ask you questions about your risk aversion, timeline, growth goals, net worth, and can then present and suggest the types of holdings that match your answers. They can walk you through their website and answer additional questions. You can provide input into how you want your money invested and your Advisor should help you direct your investments accordingly. You will be able to view your account online or on a phone app whenever you like.

Note that having a financial advisor or money manager does not mean you have enlisted a wizard who you can count on to accurately predict what will happen with your money. They are not trained to hit home runs for you. They are educated in their field and know how to navigate the markets and invest your money, based on *your* goals.

Financial Advisor(s) are in the financial and investment knowledge business as a career, and their proficiency level will be difficult for the average person to match. With that said, many

---

[48] Tristan Reddy, "Asset Manager vs. Financial Advisor," Carmague, November 10, 2023, https://www.camargueum.co.za/asset-manager-vs-financial-advisor/#:~:text=While%20an%20asset%20manager%20allocates,purely%20to%20earn%20investmen t%20returns.

investors prefer to have control of their own account as well as to avoid paying Advisor fees and commissions.

## Managing Your Own Investment Portfolio

No one cares more about your finances than you do. You may be motivated to invest on your own, without the help of an Advisor, through education, the brokerage website and available investing tools, blogs, podcasts, and finance shows. There is no rule against using this tactic and many investors choose this path. You are free to invest on your own, and you might already have a good idea as to how you're going to proceed. Keep in mind that building your fortune *successfully* is of paramount importance. You will want to keep a very close eye on your investments if you plan to oversee them.

## A Hybrid Approach

If you're just starting out on your investing journey, even if your wish is to manage your own finances, you are encouraged to begin with an advisor to at least become confident, gain knowledge, and develop your prowess. Would this strategy help to give you confidence that you're starting your investing 'career' in a proper direction? You can always decide on other options down the road.

No matter how you decide to begin this journey, don't delay!

Investment Options:

Your investment choices are countless! You may pick from among many ideas, the most popular being the Stock Market. While more people may own Real Estate than stocks, fewer make their Real Estate purchases primarily for investment purposes. Other choices aside from the Stock Market and Real Estate include precious metals such as Gold, Silver, Coins and Currency, collectibles including Rare Automobiles, Artwork, Figurines, Sports Cards and Memorabilia, and a myriad of untold other popular treasures. CDs are safer investments, and High Yield (higher interest paying) Savings Accounts are becoming more popular. You might choose to invest in your own new business. Your choices are truly limitless.

If you plan to invest in the markets, (for our purposes, the word 'market' or 'markets' will signify both the stock and bond markets), investing can be as simple as you like. You have the option to set up automatic investing that executes and goes toward a pre-selected group of holdings each time your bank transfer hits, without needing action from you. You can carry on with your day and life as if nothing happened, knowing your new savings are automatically going toward investments you have chosen. You can also choose to be in charge and handle your own trades, which requires more attention and diligence.

If the markets are not for you, you'll now begin pursuing your other investment options, such as which property to purchase, the rare coins you wish to buy, or your other ideas. This is the beginning of the makeover and elevation of your financial life!

If using the markets, you might know where you plan to direct your monthly fistfuls of dollars. For others who are new to the investing world, a logical question is "What should I invest in?" The all-important answers to this question will depend on many factors, including your soon-to-be blooming investing style, the economy, your knowledge level and your risk tolerance. The markets are the most well-known and popular investments.

If you are contributing all your savings to your company's 401k, then you have an assortment of options including mutual funds (groups of stocks or bonds) that you can choose from. You can spread your investments and risk over multiple of these funds if you like.

Those with access to a 401k plan have an excellent investing avenue for multiple reasons. The income you invest is not taxed until you retire and begin withdrawing it, therefore your money can grow uninterrupted for many years. Also, the company that you work for will typically contribute an additional percentage of (free!) money into your fund depending on how much you invest! This can be huge in helping your portfolio compound and grow! Always try to contribute at least enough to receive the full company match. It's not often that someone offers you free money!

Another advantage to having a company 401k plan; Should you ever need to access your funds prior to retirement, it's possible to easily borrow money from your own account. And there's a nice bonus, as you would be borrowing from yourself <u>interest-free</u>, since it's your money! While it's debt and you will have to pay it back, there are no interest charges!

If you don't have access to a 401K plan via your company, then you will have the freedom to create and contribute to your own Traditional or Roth IRA, (or Keough Plan if you are self-employed or a small business owner). These plans also offer tax advantages versus simply investing your cash on your own. Differences between IRAs:

| TRADITIONAL IRA | ROTH IRA |
|---|---|
| You contribute with pretax dollars | You contribute with after-tax dollars |
| Can deduct contributions from your taxes if you qualify | Cannot deduct contributions from your taxes |
| Removing initial contributions can lead to taxes and a penalty | Can withdraw initial contributions at any time without taxes or a penalty |
| Features required minimum distributions | No required minimum distributions[49] |

---

[49] Jean Murray, "What Is A Traditional IRA?", The Balance, September 27, 2022, https://www.thebalancemoney.com/what-is-a-traditional-ira-and-who-should-have-one-1289861#:~:text=Example%20of%20a%20Traditional%20IRA,-

History provides us with a snapshot of the average annual long-term performance of various investment choices you will have to select from. The next chapter will provide some insight on much of that performance to help you have a feel and comfort level for what to invest in.

If you like to read, a finance book or two would be a good new hobby for a beginning investor, or anyone for that matter. My 21-year-old son pleasantly surprised me recently by purchasing two new books on investing. All our kids are investing at an early age. I have a good feeling that they are all on a promising path to success!

One common investing motto that will help to prevent you from suffering big losses; *Spread your risk out!* Don't sink your entire savings into one or two investments. We have all heard stories of people who have lost their entire fortunes. We don't want those stories to be written about us. Many financial experts would agree and advise that **no more than 5% or 10% of your retirement savings should ever go into any specific investment.**

Now it's time to have the talk. You know, 'the talk.' How will *your* investments perform? Over your investing career, you will experience good or great periods as well as painful times. No one, not even the most brilliant financial minds on earth, can accurately predict what tomorrow brings. Thus, the concept of spreading your risk out across multiple areas can help keep you from having a catastrophic loss.

The economy is ever changing, and while there will be periods of excellent growth, or bull markets, we will all likely experience multiple extended downturns (bear markets) recessions or worse during our working careers, which would mean a period of falling values affecting your investment account negatively.

Periods of growth (bull markets) are most prevalent! Consider the following numbers when comparing bull and bear markets. The

---

Suppose%20you're&text=You%20decide%20to%20put%20%246%2C000,funds%2C%20or%20other%20similar%20securities.

average length of a bear (falling value) market is 292 days, or about 9.7 months. That's significantly shorter than the average length of a bull market, (rising value), which is 992 days or 2.7 years.[50] **Stocks lose 35% on average in a bear market. By contrast, stocks gain 114% on average during a bull market.**[51] This data helps to explain and support the excellent growth in the stock market since its inception.

Keep in mind the historic growth numbers of what you're invested in. What goes down has always recovered and then some when it comes to the stock market. This also supports the 'buy and hold' concept, especially when you consider the number of years you could have your money invested.

With respect to your portfolio, market performance today, tomorrow, next month, or next year is not as crucial when compared to how your investments perform over *your time horizon*, that is until you wish to begin using your retirement funds. Therefore, unless you plan to retire in just a few years, the growth history of the markets over time should be on your side.

The complete spectrum of how investors choose to invest is diverse. On one end of the scale are those who use the strategy of 'buy and hold,' selecting and then leaving their investments alone, counting on the long-term annual average growth in the markets. In the middle of the spectrum are those who like to shuffle their

---

[50] "10 Things You Should Know About Bear Markets, Hartford Funds, November 10, 2023, https://www.hartfordfunds.com/practice-management/client-conversations/managing-volatility/bear-markets.html#:~:text=Bear%20markets%20tend%20to%20be,average%20frequency%20between%20bear%20markets.

[51] "10 Things You Should Know About Bear Markets, Hartford Funds, November 10, 2023, https://www.hartfordfunds.com/practice-management/client-conversations/managing-volatility/bear-markets.html#:~:text=Bear%20markets%20tend%20to%20be,average%20frequency%20between%20bear%20markets.

investments around, and time market movement (buy low, sell high) watching and trading as conditions change. On the other end of the span are the day traders who attempt to buy and sell shares regularly, letting their smaller gains add up.

Many 'buy and hold' strategists like to collect from dividend paying stocks. Some mutual funds (a group of stocks or bonds) and stocks will pay you money in the form of a 'Dividend' every quarter just for owning them, regardless of their performance. The dividend is equivalent to a bonus. You can either take the dividend payments in cash, or better yet you can choose to have that money reinvested right back into your account where it can take advantage of compounding growth.

What is the benefit of a dividend paying fund or stock? Let's say the company or mutual fund you're investing in pays you an average dividend of 3% each year that you own it. Now let's suppose that the fund or stock remains flat in value during a particular year. You still grew by 3% thanks to that dividend! So, let's take that same fund or stock, and in another year, its value increases by 10%. Your total growth during that year is now 13%, as you were able to double dip both the growth and dividend! It follows that even in a losing year for dividend paying stocks, your account won't recede as much because you're getting that dividend percentage and payment to offset the loss.

If you want to learn more about reliable companies that have a long history of paying dividends, research the 'Dividend Aristocrats' and 'Dividend Kings'. These companies have a history of continuously paying a growing dividend, (at least 25 years consecutively for the Aristocrats and 50 years for the Kings), making them among the safer and more popular stock investments.

You will find some very familiar company names among the Dividend Aristocrats and Kings. There are even mutual funds available containing all or many of the companies that are classified as Dividend Aristocrats and Kings.

As your nest egg grows, its importance to you will increase. You won't want to lose a large portion of what you have worked much of your life to save. Most people approaching their retirement years will want to move their money into safer investments and begin reducing risk. Work with your advisor or if you are managing your own investments, have a plan for your career and lifetime!

Some of you may not want to invest at all. Saving your money without investing is a strategy that many people pursue and is virtually risk free! It is also virtually growth free. On top of that, inflation reduces the value of your savings, making non-invested/non-growing money *lose value* over time. Still, it is your money, and saving involves little to no risk. It's always your choice!

If you choose to save and want your savings to <u>grow</u> while in your bank, you can earn interest via putting your cash into CD's or high yield savings banks!

One could also opt for a mixture of sorts and invest a percentage of their money and keep the balance in a savings or checking account with lower risk. (Don't forget the emergency fund...).

Regardless of how you manage your money over your career, if you *are* saving, be proud to be in that fortunate camp and give yourself a congratulatory pat on the back.

Our next chapter dives deeper into the <u>performance history</u> of many of your choices in the stock market, bond market, and other popular investment options.

# Chapter 21:
# Cheat Sheet: Historic Growth Rates Of Popular Investment Options

*"We can learn from our past."*

Whether you're just starting on your investing journey, or if you're adding to what you've already saved, you'll now have the added comfort of growing security and flexibility for you and your family.

An evolving retirement account with your name on it is emerging. As you begin making the all-important selections of what to invest in, it may be helpful to know how the investment options you're considering have grown in the past.

This chapter attempts to provide a sort of 'cheat sheet' for you to get acquainted with investment categories. We share how various types of investments have performed over time, and you may soon agree that most of them have done quite well! Even so, the first one million rules about investing are: *Nothing is guaranteed, ever!* No investment is guaranteed, and certainly no advice from anyone on what to invest in is guaranteed. There's an old saying that if something is too good to be true, then it probably is. That saying no doubt originated from an investor who took advice on a 'sure thing'.

Let's take a trip back in time, to an earlier page for a moment with a reminder of the 7-1/2% annual growth percentage that this book uses to project your investment growth potential. That number is for **the 'stock market' which has grown an average of 10% per year since 1929, even considering the great depression and recessions our country has endured.** [52]

---

[52] James Royal, Ph.D., Arielle O'Shea, "What Is The Average Stock Market Return?", NerdWallet, September 14, 2023, https://www.nerdwallet.com/article/investing/average-stock-market-return

If you prefer to use another annual growth percentage for any type investment, no problem! You can calculate your projection by visiting us at findyourhiddentreasurechest.com or by using any of the numerous online calculators available. It's simple and straightforward to calculate how much money we can have in the future if we make a specific monthly or annual contribution at a projected interest rate over time. Simply input your monthly contribution, the length of time in years you will provide it, and your preferred interest (growth) rate. Boom, you'll get your future projection!

What will *your* annual growth rate be? That is yet to be determined and will be influenced by numerous factors, *including what you invest in.* As we've discussed, some will out-perform the historic averages, and others will fall short, depending on the 'who, what, where, when, how, and why' you invest.

You may surmise from some of the upcoming data that it's quite possible to average 10-12% or more in annual growth. History may prove you to be correct! However, as you move closer to retirement age, you should work to ensure the safety of the portfolio that you have devoted decades of effort to create and build. As the years roll by and the size of your account increases, you may use the common strategy of gradually moving into less risky investment types. Those holdings might provide lower annual returns, but you will surely sleep better, knowing your vault of future enjoyment is safer.

**Let's review the historic averages of some of the most popular investment types including the stock market and bond exchanges and indexes, real estate and banking investments, along with the historic average annual performance of each. If any of these are confusing, have these pages ready when you speak with your advisor. He or she will be able to clarify:**

## STOCKS

Stocks consist of all of the shares into which ownership of a corporation or company is divided. A single share of the stock means fractional ownership of the corporation in proportion to the total number of shares. These stocks are purchased on the stock market where buyers and sellers exchange equity shares of public corporations. **While each year can differ greatly, the stock market has averaged 10% annual growth over the past century.**[53]

**Mutual Funds and ETFs:** Stocks can be purchased together in groups reducing risk. A mutual fund is a professionally managed investment fund that pools money from many investors to purchase securities. The term is typically used in the United States, Canada, and India, while similar structures across the globe include the SICAV in Europe and open-ended investment company in the UK.[54]

Mutual funds can be bought and sold **directly from the company that manages them, from an online discount broker, or from a full-service broker.** Information you need to choose a fund is online at the financial company websites, online broker sites, and financial news websites.[55]

For stock mutual funds, a "good" long-term return (annualized, for 10 years or more) is **8% to 10%.** For bond mutual funds, a good long-term return would be **4% to 5%.**[56]

**'ETFs or "exchange-traded funds"** are exactly as the name implies: **funds that trade on exchanges, generally tracking a specific index.** When you invest in an ETF, you get a bundle of assets

---

[53] James Royal, Ph.D., Arielle O'Shea, "What Is The Average Stock Market Return?", NerdWallet, September 14, 2023, https://www.nerdwallet.com/article/investing/average-stock-market-return

[54] "Mutual Fund," Wikipedia, November 10, 2023, https://en.wikipedia.org/wiki/Mutual_fund

[55] "Mutual Fund," Wikipedia, November 10, 2023, https://en.wikipedia.org/wiki/Mutual_fund

[56] Kent Thume, "What Is A Good Annual Return For A Mutual Fund?", The Balance, November 20, 2021, https://www.thebalancemoney.com/good-annual-mutual-fund-return-4767418

you can buy and sell during market hours—potentially lowering your risk and exposure, while helping to diversify your portfolio.'[57]

'For Exchange Traded Funds, the average ETF return of an S&P 500 index is **11.82%** since inception.[58] Average ETF returns vary, but on average, you should expect to generate an annualized return of **7-10%** over a ten-year period.'[59]

The two major U.S. stock exchanges are the NYSE and Nasdaq. There are also well-known indexes which measure specific groups of stocks. The largest are the S & P 500, the Dow Jones, and the Nasdaq composite. Note that there are also smaller exchanges and index funds. The annual average performance for each of the above is shown in two ways: since inception, and over the past 10 years, (to give you a comparison as well as a more realistic picture of achievement during current times).

**Dow Jones:** A measure of thirty of the most prominent corporations in America. Annual growth since inception: **8.70%**[60] Last 10 years: **10.68%**[61]

**S & P 500:** The Standard and Poor's 500, or simply the S&P 500, is a stock market index tracking the stock performance of 500 of the

---

[57] David Koenig, CFA®, FRM®, "Understanding ETF's and Dividends," Charles Schwab, December 9, 2019, https://intelligent.schwab.com/article/understanding-etfs-and-dividends

[58] Josh Smith, "Blog Post #77", Themarkethustle.com, December 2, 2022, https://www.themarkethustle.com/news/average-etf-return-how-much-will-you-make

[59] Josh Smith, "Blog Post #77", Themarkethustle.com, December 2, 2022, https://www.themarkethustle.com/news/average-etf-return-how-much-will-you-make

**60** Kent Thume, "What Is The Average Return of the Market?" Seeking Alpha.com, January 2, 2023, https://seekingalpha.com/article/4502739-average-stock-market-return

[61] Lance Cothern, "What is the Historical Average Stock Market Return?" My Bank Tracker, January 4, 2023, https://www.mybanktracker.com/blog/investing/average-stock-market-return-302399

largest companies listed on stock exchanges in the United States. It is one of the most commonly followed equity indices.[62] The index has returned a historic annualized average return of around **11.88%** since its 1957 inception through the end of 2021.[63] Last 10 years: **10.90%**[64]

**Nasdaq:** Overall: The Nasdaq 100 index has generated an average annual return between **15% – 17%** over the past 38 years.[65] Last 10 years: **14.39%**[66]

## BONDS

A bond is a type of security under which the issuer owes the holder a debt and is obliged – depending on the terms – to repay the principal of the bond at the maturity date as well as interest over a specified amount of time.    Interest is usually payable at fixed intervals.[67] (Worded another way, you're the banker and you are loaning your money to the government, or a corporation or corporations and you're being paid interest). **In general, there are three ways you can buy bonds:**

- Buying newly issued individual bonds directly from a borrower.

---

[62] "S & P 500," Wikipedia, November 10, 2023, https://en.wikipedia.org/wiki/S%26P_500

[63] J. B. Maverick, "S & P 500 Average Return," Investopedia, May 24, 2023, https://www.investopedia.com/ask/answers/042415/what-average-annual-return-sp-500.asp

[64] Lance Cothern, "What is the Historical Average Stock Market Return?" My Bank Tracker, January 4, 2023, https://www.mybanktracker.com/blog/investing/average-stock-market-return-302399

[65] Abheey, "Nasdaq – 100 Historical Annual Returns, (1986-2023)," Finasko, September 22,2023, https://finasko.com/nasdaq-100-returns/

[66] Lance Cothern, "What is the Historical Average Stock Market Return?" My Bank Tracker, January 4, 2023, https://www.mybanktracker.com/blog/investing/average-stock-market-return-302399

[67] "Bond (Finance)," Wikipedia, November 10, 2023, https://en.wikipedia.org/wiki/Bond_(finance)

- Buying new or existing individual bonds through your brokerage account.

- Buying bond mutual funds or exchange-traded funds.[68]

Since 1926, long-term government bonds have returned between **5%** and **6%**, according to investment researcher Morningstar. The average annual rate over the past 10 years from 2013-2022 has been **2.15%** and has been rising, nearing 5% recently.

Corporate bond rates vary widely, and in general, the higher the interest rate they pay, the riskier the investment. (Companies can go out of business or default!).

## REAL ESTATE

Investing in real estate typically carries less risk than the stock market and has traditionally offered a safer, lower annual return. The historic growth percentage of real estate purchases can vary geographically and by the type of real estate that you invest in, i.e.: land, home, rental property, commercial property.

Most families and individuals who invest in real estate purchase a home. 'House Price Index YoY (year over year, or annually) in the United States averaged 4.58 percent from 1992 until 2023, reaching an all-time high of 19.10 percent in July of 2021 and a record low of -10.60 percent in November of 2008.[69]

## BANK PRODUCTS

Within your bank there are a few investment opportunities.

---

[68] Dan Kaplinger, "How to Buy Bonds: 3 Options You Should Consider," Motley Fool, August 5, 2017, https://www.fool.com/retirement/2017/08/05/how-to-buy-bonds-3-options-you-should-consider.aspx

[69] "United States House Price Index YoY," Trading Economics, November 10, 2023, https://tradingeconomics.com/united-states/house-price-index-yoy

**Certificates of Deposit (CD's):** These rates are set like other banking rates[70] (and can be comparable or slightly lower than bond rates). Banks and credit unions often use an index rate, typically the federal funds rate (also known as the "fed funds" rate), as a base to set rates for all interest-bearing accounts. They fluctuate with inflation and the economy.'[71]

Check with your bank for more information if you're interested in investing in these products. Today, CD's range between **4 ½ to 5 ½ %**. CDs are lower risk.

**Savings Accounts:** In general banks pay a **very small fraction of 1%** interest to your savings and checking accounts. Savings accounts generally are not considered 'investments.' There are, however, 'high yield' savings accounts available from numerous sources. These offer to pay more than standard banking savings accounts (2-3-4% today) and remain lower risk. These rates will vary.

**Money markets:** A safe low interest investment option. 'The money market involves the purchase and sale of large volumes of very short-term debt products, such as overnight reserves or commercial paper.'[72] Money market rates are typically slightly higher than savings bank interest rates. 'By investing in a money market fund, which may often yield just 2% or 3% due to the fixed income nature of its investments, an investor may be missing out on an opportunity for a better rate of return.'[73]

---

[70] "Bank Products," Finra, November 10, 2023, https://www.finra.org/investors/investing/investment-products/bank-products

[71] "Bank Products," Finra, November 10, 2023, https://www.finra.org/investors/investing/investment-products/bank-products

[72] Adam Hayes, "Money Markets: What They Are, How They Work, and Who Uses Them," Investopedia, June 20, 2023, https://www.investopedia.com/terms/m/moneymarket.asp

[73] Glenn Curtis, "Money Market Funds: Advantages and Disadvantages," Investopedia, June 19, 2023, https://www.investopedia.com/articles/mutualfund/08/money-market.asp#:~:text=Over%20time%2C%20common%20stocks%20have,a%20better%20rate%20of%20return.

## ANNUITIES

'The term "annuity" refers to an insurance contract issued and distributed by financial institutions with the intention of paying out invested funds in a fixed income stream in the future. Investors invest in or purchase annuities with monthly premiums or lump-sum payments. The holding institution issues a stream of payments in the future for a specified period or for the remainder of the annuitant's life. Annuities are mainly used for retirement purposes and help individuals address the risk of outliving their savings.74 There can be many variables with respect to how annuities are paid, and they are dependent on current interest rates. The debates on the value of annuities cover the entire spectrum. Current rates are near the 5% number. Rates will vary.

## CRYPTOCURRENCY

'A cryptocurrency, crypto-currency, crypto, or coin is a digital currency designed to work as a medium of exchange through a computer network that is not reliant on any central authority, such as a government or bank, to uphold or maintain it.'[75]

Some online brokers offer access to cryptocurrencies, which are generally considered high risk, high reward.

I hope this concise overview of the more popular or 'mainstream' investment choices has provided a little clarity. Please seek out a professional or expert in the areas that you are interested in investing in.

---

[74] Julia Kagan, "Guide to Annuities; What They Are, Types and How They Work," Investopedia, March 30, 2023, https://www.investopedia.com/terms/a/annuity.asp

[75] "Cryptocurrency," Wikipedia, November 10, 2023, https://en.wikipedia.org/wiki/Cryptocurrency

What may be more important than how you invest is the fact that you *are investing*. *Most of America's wealth was created through investing, so you must be on the right track!*

# Chapter 22:
# Monitor Your Growth And Always Look For Ways To Add

*"It's easy to remember your money."*

You now have new motion in your financial life. So, what's next? Do you go on with your career and wait for a sign from above that tells you your retirement account is ready for you? Of course not! Your investments are very important. There are a few things that you can and should keep an eye on that will help to ensure the growth and success of your portfolio.

There are at least two occurrences in the future that will allow you to increase your contribution amount. First, whenever your income increases, your next thought (after "Yippee!") should be how much you can add to your monthly investment allocation.

Secondly, you will want to analyze your bills and expenses often. Make a note on your calendar to review your situation quarterly, or whatever makes sense to you. Be your own coach and look for opportunities so you can add to your monthly savings deposits.

Future reviews will be a shorthand version of the savings exercise you just went through. Keep your finances tight and ensure you're not overpaying for anything unnecessarily.

The continuing goal is to ADD SAVINGS TO YOUR CURRENT MONTHLY AMOUNT. If you add to your monthly savings annually, your chances of achieving and surpassing your dream and goal will be high! Have confidence that if you continuously add to what you've started here, your outcome could provide some BIG options for you, such as retiring with significant wealth or even retiring early!

Another great ally for the success of your investment account will be education. Whether you enlist the help of a professional or plan to rely on your own knowledge, research and education can assist you in keeping and growing, vs. losing what you are saving. Isn't that goal #1?

You should check your account often. The phone app makes this simple! Your portfolio can experience incredible runs of exciting growth, as well as enduring economic downturns and a recession or two. There is a 'caveat emptor' around every corner when it comes to your money, and now is a good time to re-assert that while you will have some thrilling days of, investing will not be all unicorns and skittles.

At any time, you have the option to sell some or all of your investments, converting them to cash or a low-risk money market account. If you're uncomfortable investing at any time, you can simply stop for a while. That also carries the risk of missing out on growth. But there are investors who move in and out of cash positions as they wait for lower-priced bargains before buying back in. I am not suggesting this for you, rather I am letting you know that you don't need to be invested every day if you choose not to.

Everyone watches their money. The very best of luck monitoring yours as your net worth and future become more exciting!

# Chapter 23:
# Summary

*"Be proud that you took action."*

The key to most of America's wealth is through investing. While the common mantra and school of thought may be that investing is a treat that is reserved only for the rich, you have just employed a system for saving and investing money that can benefit virtually anyone.

Investing was never meant to be an exclusive club or playground. Anyone can partake, but to begin requires the ability to save money. Therein lies the difficulty for nearly half of America today.

You have enacted a more manageable, less painful method of saving that can help people who typically have found saving to be painful, thereby making a comfortable future more possible.

If you have taken part in this exercise, you have found your map and followed its 'clues' leading to your own hidden treasure chest. You've initiated on your own a treasure chest that contains the seeds of growing wealth that will bloom over time.

You've solved your investment puzzle in a unique way by finding and giving yourself a 'pay raise'. You've found a way to suddenly begin saving and investing money without the typical need for personal sacrifice such as adding a second job or giving up favorite activities or luxuries in your life. This is a method with which you can stick!

You have initiated (or increased) your monthly savings contribution by safely having it deposited each month directly into your (newly created) investment account or other investments.

You are living proof that you don't have to be rich to be an investor or to have hope for a more comfortable and secure future. You've plugged leaking holes in your expenses, and you've put that money to work by first eliminating your debt if needed, and then by directing it into your investment account, growing for you and your family's future and retirement.

Saving is about to become a habit for you. It's really no big deal. It's the same as paying a bill, *and you are putting away money for later that can become more rewarding and valuable to you than most of the things you're spending your money on!*

Remember how important saving and investing is. This is the first big step to changing your circumstances. The rest is up to you. You'll need to be diligent and *stick with your plan.*

Add to your monthly savings whenever possible, for the rest of your working career! Your continuing resolve will help ensure your future is as big and shiny as possible!

**Remember that no one regrets saving for their retirement. But there are many people who reach retirement age and regret <u>not</u> having saved!**

**If you have completed all the steps in this book, remembering that your retirement account is another bill you must continue to pay, there is no other outcome than saving, investing and experiencing wealth that you otherwise wouldn't have.**

So, what's going to happen with *your* retirement plan? Will it go just like you planned? Manage your expectations! While some of you might come very close to achieving your set goal, most will likely end up elsewhere on the graph, overachieving or falling short.

Regardless of your future results, you ultimately will have changed the direction in your life's financial story by adding a financial plan and you will have achieved a worthy accomplishment in your lifetime. Let yourself dream big, be excited at your possibilities!

You are adding much more than money to your life. Security, confidence, better relationships, pride and a legacy can all be a part of your future. Speaking of that legacy, if you have children remember the effect your example as an investor and provider can have on their futures. It could be one of your *greatest gifts!* Pass on what you have learned, instill this worthy habit in your next generation, and they can teach future generations to come. The lessons *you* provide can elevate the future of your family to another level!

Keep this book handy! You may want to return to it as you search for additional savings. Situations change. You'll hopefully enjoy a rising income throughout your working career. The savings plan you enact will be a 'living, breathing plan' that you can review, add to, and change whenever the situation dictates.

No matter where your investment savings and future ultimately land, you will have the opportunity for more of the things we all dream of; to live a more comfortable life, to travel, for higher education, to ensure your spouse and family's security, to donate to your heartfelt cause, to retire in greater comfort and with less worry, and perhaps with an estate and legacy to leave to your family.

In addition to all that you will have created and built in your lifetime, this account is *yours*, and is the hidden treasure chest that you have found and uncovered through your own initiative and hard work.

Anyone *can* be an investor! Anyone can establish the *great habit* of saving and investing to enrich their brighter future. My wish for you is a more promising and successful life. Dream big, stick to your plan, and wishing you the very best of success!

---

## 'One Small Action' (Cont'd)

*Your retirement ceremony is memorable. Friends tell stories and share memories. Many of them ask you what you will do now that you have retired. You share the vacations you have already planned, as well as improvements you are designing for your home. You comment that there might be a boat acquisition soon. You can't help but notice some 'oohs' and 'aahs.'*

*As the party ends and you are on your way out the door, you stop and turn to take one last look around the room, and you pause, reminiscing on some of the unforgettable memories. You reflect again on how grateful you are that you took the actions you did way back when...the feeling is euphoric and almost overtakes you.*

*You are reaping the rewards for having created the treasure chest of wealth that will serve all your coming needs. You and your family are looking forward to an exciting future ahead.*

*You smile as you close the door and walk off into the sunset, excited for the next chapter...*

# APPENDIX A: Sample and Additional Worksheet

## SAVINGS WORKSHEET (SAMPLE)

PROJECTED NUMBER OF YEARS TO RETIREMENT ___40___

RETIREMENT GOAL ___$1,000,000___

| OPPORTUNITY AND NOTES | PROJ MO SAVINGS | TOT PROJ MO SVGS | PROJ LT SAVINGS | TOT PROJ LT SVGS |
|---|---|---|---|---|
| Cell Phone | $15 | $15 | $42,312 | $42,312 |
| Cut Drive Thru Coffee | 100 | 115 | 281,978 | 324.272 |
| Reduce Thermostat | 9 | 124 | 25,3943 | 49,648 |
| Reduce Auto Ins Payment | 16 | 140 | 45,1323 | 94,762 |
| Cut Grocery Expense | 20 | 160 | 56,4104 | 51,154 |
| Cut Restaurant Exp/Appetizer | 30 | 190 | 84,6065 | 35,742 |
| Bag Lunch From Now On | 120 | 310 | 338,370 | 874,093 |
| Cut Our Dog's Hair (est. $50) | 50 | 360 | 140,998 | 1,015,073 |

## AUTO TRANSFER AMOUNT MONTHLY: $360_____ I think
is realistic which projects to $1,015,073 in 40 years! I will review and try to add every year!

# SAVINGS WORKSHEET

PROJECTED NUMBER OF YEARS TO RETIREMENT _____

RETIREMENT GOAL $_____

| OPPORTUNITY AND NOTES | PROJ MO SAVINGS | TOT PROJ MO SVGS | PROJ LT SAVINGS | TOT PROJ LT SVGS |
|---|---|---|---|---|
| | | | | |
| | | | | |
| | | | | |
| | | | | |
| | | | | |
| | | | | |
| | | | | |
| | | | | |
| | | | | |
| | | | | |
| | | | | |
| | | | | |
| | | | | |
| | | | | |
| | | | | |

**TOTAL TO TRANSFER TO INV ACCT MONTHLY:**       $_____

# APPENDIX B:

Visit our website for savings worksheets, valuable tools and ideas!

findyourhiddentreasurechest.com

# Acknowledgments

There are not enough thanks available for my wife Carol who helped me to stay on track and for the countless think tank sessions; for being a soundboard; and for creating an environment of support every day to help me stumble to the finish line.

Thank you for the special guidance along the way to my friend, A.R. Elia, author, and screenwriter. Check out his enjoyable novels, 'Opening Round, The Tournament' and 'Telegraph' on Amazon and at astorpress.com, or at your local bookstore.

Thank you to those who helped pre-screen and add value to this idea before its release: Bob, Gary and Rick. Your advice provided priceless direction, insight and clarity!

# About the Author

Matt Simmons makes his literary debut with 'Find Your Hidden Treasure Chest,' a self-help work offering uncomplicated, sustainable financial wealth building advice to the masses.

Matt has a B.S. degree in Business Administration as well as being experienced in correspondence, analysis, and quality assurance during his time served in the US Navy. He also spent 30 years in the surgical device field in Sales and Management.

Matt has owned and sold one small business, and currently spends his time firing and rehiring himself while running two newer small companies. He also enjoys golfing, boating, fishing, and traveling, along with his love of writing. Matt and his wife Carol live in south Florida and have three successful adult children living in the southeast United States.

0c3bc956-6fd1-4325-8ebd-552034f2cb46R01